Life Is
Eternal Newness

Ilie Cioara

Life Is
Eternal Newness

BOOKS

Winchester, UK
Washington, USA

First published by O-Books, 2012
O-Books is an imprint of John Hunt Publishing Ltd., Laurel House, Station Approach,
Alresford, Hants, SO24 9JH, UK
office1@o-books.net
www.o-books.com

For distributor details and how to order please visit the 'Ordering' section on our website.

Text copyright: Ilie Cioara, Petrica Verdes 2011

thesilencebook.blogspot.com

ISBN: 978 1 78099 097 2

A CIP catalogue record for this book is available from the British Library.

Translation by Petrica Verdes

Design: Lee Nash

Printed and bound by CPI Group (UK) Ltd., Croydon, CR0 4YY
Printed in the USA by Offset Paperback Mfrs, Inc

We operate a distinctive and ethical publishing philosophy in all
areas of our business, from our global network of authors to
production and worldwide distribution.

CONTENTS

Introduction

All the poems in this volume tackle one and the same subject: "Knowing oneself". Every title represents a different perspective on Life in Its eternal unfoldment, attempting to reveal Its mysteries and Its real meaning.

Each poem represents a true mirror, a gift from the author to the reader, with the invitation to look into it and see yourself, in simplicity, the same way you would glance at your face in an ordinary mirror. Just watch, with a clear, lucid, totally passive mind! The simplicity of this encounter is devoid of purpose, expectation or any form of duality.

Everything we encounter in this manner, such as thoughts, images, desires, emotions etc. completely disappears, without leaving any memory residues. In the "psychological void" that ensues, the conditioned mind disappears and we expand into Infinity; we attain a new mind, dimensionless and all-encompassing. In this state, we are endowed with the capacity to embrace and comprehend the eternity of the present moment.

If – while reading one of the poems – you experience the sphere of the Infinite as a state of Pure Consciousness, the merit for this encounter is solely yours. Straight away, in that very moment, break the mirror and throw away all the shards so that nothing is left of it! Do not accumulate the experience in the memory. Any attempts to store it for subsequent use only fortify the imaginary structure of the "ego". If, nevertheless, as a result of a lack of Attention, you have burdened yourself with the memory of the experience, you can eliminate it only through a simple and direct encounter, without pursuing anything in particular.

This message, expressed in very simple words, invites you to watch yourself, in every circumstance, as often as possible. Each such encounter – performed in the right manner – constantly weakens the authority of the "ego".

Attention – as a shining Light – dissipates all the darkness, dissolving and disintegrating everything it encounters, like a laser. We don't memorize anything from the poem we have just read or re-read. In this way, the verses will be always new – completely unknown to us – as if we are reading them for the first time; just like, when you look into a mirror, you see your face in it as if for the first time.

The passiveness of the mind, as a result of all-encompassing and lucid Attention, transcends us from the finite world into the reality of the Absolute, revealing our true divine origin. Completely forget the poems, as well as the author! Just remain with the constant act of listening and watching yourself, in utter simplicity.

You don't need anyone or anything on this path of spiritual awakening! Drop all the crutches you rely on, for they are worthless! On the contrary, they are real obstacles on this wondrous journey, which can only be accomplished in the absence of the "ego", in utter aloneness, as a complete human being, body and mind as "One".

In order to better understand how this Wholeness becomes manifest, we must mention that, in a state of humble stillness of the mind, our being is absorbed into the Sphere of the Infinite – where thinking cannot enter. Here, in total melting with the Source of all Sources, we are creative Love and we manifest ourselves as such, renewing ourselves moment to moment.

What we describe here are not mere theories or imaginary concepts about Life, but true facts, verifiable from personal experience, as you read or listen to one of the poems. The carefully chosen words are nothing but mere indicators. Their only purpose is to invite us to listen and watch – in a certain manner – both the reactions of the conditioned mind, as well as all the noises coming from the external world. The words merely point to a direct experience revealing Reality, which absorbs all of our self-importance.

The repetition of certain words is unavoidable; nevertheless, the experience of the reality behind the words will be always new. This encounter with Truth, in the passiveness of the mind, in the alive and active present, is a message suggesting a new way of approaching Life.

The verse, written in simple words, gives you clear guidance, inviting you to immediately apply it. Simply reading or listening to it, with a clear, attentive and lucid mind, gives you the possibility of experiencing firsthand the Reality expressed in verse.

As the individual mind becomes completely silent, it transcends into Infinity. From now on we have a new mind, boundless and timeless, free from any problems. Living in moments of existence exposes the superficial mind, the realm of the "personal self" or the "ego". By melting with the simplicity of the verse, this fiction – a creation of time – slowly starts to lose its authority. The prison is weakened and, one day, it finally collapses, dissipating its energies.

When this fortunate phenomenon occurs, the Reality of our being – eternal and immortal – takes over our whole being, guiding us through intuitive impulses. This is the new man, with a new mentality imbued with an all-encompassing Love without cause. In fact, this is the true purpose of the incarnated human being: the demolition of the old man, ruled by the tyranny of the "ego", and the affirmation of the new man, as Divinity, sufficient unto Itself.

Ilie Cioara

Life Is Eternal Becoming

Life is Energy, a Process of becoming, on renewing,
                          unfolding moments,
It has no beginning, no end – a changing permanence;
It was not created by anyone, It comes from Eternity
And flows towards Eternity, in perfect harmony.

We can also name it God or the Absolute Truth,
A word which defines its Essence and content,
Existent in Everything and Everyone, seen or unseen,
One Reality, as a creative movement.

Life in Its becoming is constant evolution,
It is never trapped by conditions, it cannot be measured,
It simply exists – as an obvious Reality,
Demonstrating, through itself, that It is perennial.

The Life of the Aliveness within us – our real being
A Divine Particle, a potential in Itself,
Always urging us to aim for Perfection
Tied to a body of flesh and to an imperfect mind.

A constant work with all the confusing aspects
Created by erroneous education and ignorant behavior
Is the inherent condition, practically enabling us
To experience "That which is pure and evident".

***

All these fantasies disappear, without effort or struggle,
When we encounter them attentively, without any
resistance,
They are empty images, deceitful delusions,
They have no support through themselves, as
self-sustaining energies.

Let us nevertheless bless them, for they are necessary,
Let us know ourselves – our creative being,
Real Divinity, manifesting itself as Beauty, Kindness,
Joy, Happiness – melting as one.

Life is Energy in a permanent process of renewal, unfolding moment to moment. It has no beginning and it will never have an end. It comes from Eternity and it flows, perpetually, towards the same Eternity, in a perfectly harmonious order.

We can also call it Absolute Truth or God; these words define its Essence and content as All there is, in All and Everything, seen or unseen.

As Unique Reality, It is also endowed with creative force, and the Aliveness within us represents the Divine Spark which cannot be conditioned or measured, searched for or evaluated. It exists – purely and simply – as obvious and Unique Reality in a continuous process of evolution.

This Divine Particle – Perfection in Itself – is associated with a physical body and an imperfect mind; It permanently pursues perfection and the return to the Sacred Source where It originated. Destined to experience the association with the relative elements of the physical Universe, the Divine Spark – in moments of existence – comes into contact with "What is not real", that is, the world of illusions, which disappears spontaneously. In the "psychological void", It reveals Itself through Itself as Sublime Reality.

To use another form of expression, easier to understand: We can only encounter "That which is true and real" by dissipating "That which is not real", namely, the whole conditioning, as "personal self" or "ego", which dominates us psychosomatically. Therefore, only a direct encounter with the reactions of the mind: thoughts, images, desires, can enable us to discover the true "Who We really Are".

In order to experience this phenomenon, all we need is a lucid, all-encompassing, disinterested Attention. Its Light dissipates, dissolves and dispels the whole conditioning of the old man, dominating us and imposing its authority through conventional automatisms, preserved in the form of images.

Let us, therefore, bless all these shadows of the once-consumed past, for they are an opportunity to truly know our Divine Nature. This encounter with ourselves can also be called the Experience of incarnated Divinity; in this state we encounter the feelings of Joy, Kindness, Love and Happiness, as a sacred bouquet, uncontaminated and free from any form of conditioning.

Enlightenment and Describable Knowing

Enlightenment is a mystery-phenomenon, impossible
                                            to describe.
It occurs spontaneously, expanding in a new moment,
For it is eternal newness, ever-changing, moment
                                            to moment,
Whereas words are old and limited.

If we try to translate "Knowing" into words,
It ceases to be new, It becomes an imaginary opinion.
Real knowing is perceived in simplicity
By a true experiencer, as an absolute surprise.

This is Intelligence – Boundless Thinking,
Ensuing like lightning, impossible to explain;
Outdated words, recordings of the past,
Are unsuitable in the now, for they are imaginary.

A true experiencer only knows, integrated into
                                            the Absolute,
He feels no need to be recognized.
The phenomenon is experienced as a high-frequency
                                            Thought,
Preserved in the Soul, as a true reality.

8

The elevated feeling inside our being
Will attract into our Life similar absolute Thoughts,
Wisdom is recorded in the Soul,
Life becomes eternal freshness.

The pituitary gland, permanently stimulated,
Overwhelms our whole being;
The body becomes young, vital, postponing death,
Life is transformed, filled with serenity.

Love, Intelligence and compassion
Expand ceaselessly, in syntony with Wisdom,
Stimulating the being to experience higher levels
                                    of consciousness;
Finally, the seventh plane is reached.

This message represents practical information
As to what is needed; we rely only on ourselves,
In order to return to the Source, to our Home,
Through a new attitude – a holy invitation.

"Knowing" through experience and feeling,
Is your true potential and it requests of you
To expose the false – a deceitful illusion –
And to become What You Are – eternally creative Beings.

The phenomenon of Enlightenment ensues spontaneously;
by its very nature, it is mysterious and impossible to
describe. It appears as absolute newness, therefore impos-

sible to understand with the old knowing mind.

We discover Enlightenment only through feeling and experience, individually, when we truly encounter this phenomenon. It appears like a bolt of lightning and it cannot be explained using outdated words, recorded by the old mind.

The individual experiences it as an integration into the Absolute and he also feels the need to externalize it and express it. The high vibrational frequency thought which defines Enlightenment is preserved within the Soul, as a concrete memory; its essence reveals itself when this phenomenon is triggered. The feeling that created this recording will attract only very subtle Thoughts into our daily life, perpetually expanding our Wisdom. Such Thoughts stimulate the pituitary gland; it increases its hormonal mass, providing the physical body with a state of health and youth, postponing the phenomenon of death.

Peace, Harmony and serenity are undeniable effects of this reality. Love, Intelligence and Compassion in constant expansion, as well as Wisdom, stimulate and guide our being to superior levels of existence. In this manner, progressively, we will reach the seventh plane of consciousness and become one with it.

This poem-message informs us on what we need to do, by ourselves and through ourselves, in order to return to the Source of all Sources, to our home. "Self-knowing" is right in front of our eyes, inviting us to expose the false importance of the ephemeral "ego" and, through experience and feeling, to become What We truly Are, an Eternal Immortal Being. Within us all, without any exception, lies the ability to experience these hallowing attitudes and behavior.

Meditation

It cannot be trapped into patterns or models,
From the very start, it is simplicity, beyond imagination.
Thinking cannot conceive it, nor can it define it
Through methods and systems, practiced with a certain
                                        purpose or goal.

Meditation is the melting of our being into the
                                        wholeness of Life,
One with the rhythm of the Universe and its
                                        natural vibration.
It is living in the present, united with what is "now",
When the past is absent and the memory is in ashes.

When we watch ourselves attentively, the whole being
                                        is relaxed,
Just like the water of a flowing river,
In total harmony, we embrace everything naturally
And understand through Joy, as a real experience.

Integrated into Infinity, we are spontaneous Love,
We are not separated from the Hallowing Sublime.
Practically, meditation is attained in every circumstance
                                        of life,
It is not conditioned by a certain expectation.

In certain approaches, meditation is a method which, from the very beginning, imprisons us into a certain pattern, giving us assurance regarding the fulfillment of a certain result, projected in advance through an appealing image. It promises certain advantages, a certain realization on a spiritual level.

This type of meditation is dependent on a certain ambiance or atmosphere. The practitioner needs to isolate himself from the world, sit in a certain position, perform certain breathing and relaxation exercises etc.

What we describe in this poem has nothing in common with such an experience, which is and will always remain confined within the limited boundaries of the known. All that occurs in this space is implicitly created by the ignorance and deceit of the "ego".

The meditation we refer to springs from the immediate necessity – imposed by our very existence – to encounter ourselves and our erroneous way of functioning and to embrace life in its unfoldment. In order to understand what meditation is – that which appears in a flash – we need to completely free ourselves from the whole dross of the past. Only an innocent mind can embrace and comprehend the absolute newness that the flow of the aliveness brings in our path.

Faced with this stringent necessity, a natural question ensues: How can we encounter this wonderful silence, when we are, in fact, dominated by our automatic thinking process, barging into the present with its egocentric judgments and assessments?

The state of meditation itself can answer this question. It consists of listening and watching – with our full attention – each reaction of thinking appearing as a reaction to the present. In the simplicity of this encounter, we don't pursue any purpose, result or ideal and we have no expectations –

the mind becomes completely silent.

In this state of silence, we have a pure, lucid, clear consciousness, uniting us with the Great Cosmic Energy. In fact, silence allows the Sacred existent within each of us to manifest itself in all its splendor and divine infinity.

Thanks to these encounters, the vessel of consciousness, laden with residues created by egocentric energies, starts to empty itself. The simple presence of the divine within us shatters their existence, without any intervention from the practitioner.

The state of meditation we mention here can be realized in any circumstance. It is not necessary to withdraw to an isolated room, or to escape the world or to look for a particular environment. On the contrary, if practiced in the right manner, any environment is equally favorable for meditation. The contact with ourselves is real and efficient only if it is spontaneous. The attachment and detachment from our reactions is performed spontaneously and suddenly, by itself, without any will or force. All-encompassing Attention is constantly used in each encounter with "what is" in that particular moment, and it ensures the authenticity of the experience.

This is the only modality of overcoming the human condition, integrating ourselves into Universality, where we encounter the spring of Joy free from motivations, of Absolute Love and creation, operating radical transformations in the structure of the contemporary man, the so-called "Homo sapiens".

Energy and Consciousness

The Universe – all that exists – seen or unseen –
Was, is and will be – It has no beginning;
In Its essence, It is both Energy and Consciousness,
Here lies the secret of life, with its boundless knowing.

The purity of the Energy cannot be fragmented,
Consciousness, too, is an undivided unity,
Also called: God, Reality,
Limitless Love, infinite Kindness.

If we see the conditioned man as he is,
Always possessed by his fragmentary thinking,
Functioning egocentrically, in his limitedness,
Unable to understand the wondrous integration,

The surface consciousness keeps him a prisoner
Of relative energies, fearful at every step;
This is where all the conflictual states originate,
The chaos existent in the world is created by the "ego".

Living on this level, part of the Great Energy,
We are instability, a source of disharmony;
Detached from Divinity, we create our destiny,
Because of the "ego" – we drink venom from
                                        the cup of life.

Where is the salvation of the ignorant man?
It can be found within himself, when the ego is silent and
                                        newly born;
In silence, Divinity reveals itself from our depths,
The Sacred lies within every human being, appearing
                                        through simplicity.

The Boundless Universe or the Infinite, encompassing all
and everything, seen or unseen, has no beginning and it
will have no end. It has always existed; therefore it was not
created by anyone. The Source of this Unique Existence is,
therefore, Eternity; in Its perpetual movement – generated
by Itself – it flows endlessly towards one and the same
Eternity. The essence of this Boundlessness is Energy, and
Energy is also Consciousness, as the intrinsic essence of the
Aliveness.

The purity of the Energy knows no fragmentation – It
always functions as a homogeneous "Whole". Boundless
Consciousness has the same quality of functional unity.

This Consciousness or Primordial Energy can be
expressed through different symbols, such as: Cosmic
Energy, Absolute Truth, God, the Infinite, Allah, Kindness,
boundless Love, Intelligence etc.

After this brief mirroring, let us see who man is – the
master of this planet.

Because of erroneous education, the human being

detached from the real nature of his being – as divinity – and created a new identity: the surface consciousness, "personal self" or "ego". All the time-space residues, preserved in the memory, have created a being possessed by what he knows or has – as material goods and possessions. Savage egocentrism and psychological fragmentation define his mentality, isolating and closing him in the cage that he himself created. By functioning on this level, the human being is possessed by relative energies, living in conflict with himself as well as with the surrounding environment.

The chaos, ambition, violence and hatred – so obvious on the entire surface of the planet – originate in and are fueled by the dysfunctional structure of the "ego".

Detached from Divinity – as a psychologically isolated being – his day-to-day life is a permanent compromise, as well as a constant wallowing in the dark abyss of the worldly.

What possibilities of moral redemption does the conditioned man have?

First of all, he does not need any authority outside himself, because within each human being lies the Source of Life and Wisdom, inviting each individual to investigate and inquire into its reality. The revelatory action excels in its simplicity:

If the conditioned mind is humbly silent, as it realizes its powerlessness in the face of the Boundless God, what follows naturally?

In this state of no-thought – peace and psychological stillness – the Divinity within our being reveals and affirms Itself through Itself, and It overwhelms us with Its blessings. A new man appears, as an integral being, led by Love and creative Intelligence.

This Man-Love will create a new world, completely different from the world we live in at the moment.

Creation

It is never a copy, never imitation – it is perpetual
newness,
Arising from the dimension of Immensity, in a context
of life;
It cannot be created by past moments, thinking cannot
grasp it,
It is beyond mind, it has no patterns.

Creation is a surprise, affirming itself as an explosion,
Analysis cannot contain it, it excludes any comparison;
The mind often denies it, for it cannot recognize it,
It denigrates and rejects it, for it cannot understand it.

In fact, the limited can never comprehend something
outside itself:
Infinity – free from patterns;
They are worlds apart, they exclude each other,
They are different dimensions, free from conflict.

Any creation motivated by glory, fame and fortune,
Although its expression is elegant, its reality is false,
For it is possessed by time; the "self" is present in the act
of creation,
Through the channel of thinking, it conveys only
dead facts.

The alive, creative impulse appears spontaneously,
Evident uniqueness, free from any limits;
It is a burning flame, melting any bondage,
The fortunate person who encounters it becomes a
ray of light.

We can also call it Love and renewing harmony,
The human being – through feeling – is a creative flash
of light;
The whole being – alive – is a fire
Burning all: quarrel, hatred and madness.

Just watch yourselves, persistently, free from thoughts,
Only encounter concrete facts – all is solved creatively.
We create a new world; Love and harmony –
United as one – create natural kindness.

It is very difficult to find a definition of creation that is fully
satisfactory. Any such attempt will only result in a pale,
incomplete description, unable to truly explain the
phenomenon. For this reason, we will try to describe the
characteristics of the act of creation, as it is reflected in the
mirroring of the verse.

Creation is never a copy of a certain model. It is unique, it has no equal, for it is absolute, universal newness.

The human mind, based on the patterns of the past, acting from the automatic reactions of the thinking process, has no tangency with the act of creation.

Creation always appears as a lightning-like surprise and it has no comparison. This is the reason why the arrogant "ego", with its limited mind, is not only unable to understand it, but also denies or denigrates it.

This phenomenon of denial or rejection has a natural, rational and logical explanation. How could a mind, limited by the confines of knowledge, encompass and comprehend what the Universal Mind has to offer?! This truth is valid both in the case of artistic creation, as well as on a spiritual level.

The Universe reveals its mysteries and beauty only to those human beings who, through a direct experience, truly realize their powerlessness and have learned to use the key of unconditional silence.

If the mind, regardless of how cultured it may be, tries to initiate a desired act of creation, there is no way for it to accomplish such thing, as it does not have the characteristic of uniqueness that creation has.

In fact, if creation has a motivation, the end result will be a product of the past, of something already known. For instance, a painter, pursuing a personal artistic goal, tries to paint something different from his previous works. When the same painter is in a perfect state of self-oblivion, of abandonment, he paints a portrait or a landscape in a totally new and exceptional manner. That particular painting goes beyond mere technical reproduction. It is completely different from anything he has done before.

Spiritually, creation is encountered in the same climate of absence of the "ego". In that moment of perfect harmony, we are pure Energy, Love, beauty, intelligence and absolute goodness. This state of "being" is reflected in the mirror of our consciousness.

Thus, a new man is created, representing a radical transformation in the psychological structure and behavior of the contemporary man.

Each of us, through personal experience – by reaching the realm of True Love and transforming ourselves – contribute to the transformation of the entire world.

What Is Love?

In order to understand what true Love is,
We need to start the wondrous experiment with
ourselves.
The experience is simple – practice it immediately,
Just watch yourselves, in every circumstance.

The mind is unable to give a real answer,
For it is old, relative, responding from the dimension
of duality,
A bundle of feelings, deeming Love
As the opposite of hate, as similar phenomena.

True Love is, through Itself, Uniqueness,
Therefore it has no opposite! It is evident Reality,
Its nature is Divine, it is not in conflict with anything!
Kindness and Beauty are its permanent companions.

Yet, knowing what Love is – is of no use to us,
If we don't encounter it, as a living experience, in Its
                                              very nature.
Through "Self-knowing", all is revealed,
Without any "doing" or "search".

The simplicity of the encounter with the "ego"
                              in movement,
As possessive reactions – pointless and worthless –
Exposes and dissipates it; in the peace that envelops it,
The being expands, united with the Whole.

True Love appears – our Real Nature,
Part of the Divine – as an Integral Reality.
Therefore, we are Love, in any circumstance,
Everything we encounter, we just watch it as it is.

For Love defines Itself through Itself as Love,
It cleanses and transforms all that It encounters;
If we love ourselves, we see this love in everyone,
People, things and events, in their sublime unfoldment.

Ordinarily, most people use the word "love" from the level
of the conditioned mind; here, we also encounter its

opposite: hate. In this poem, as well as in the rest of the book, we do not refer to this superficial sentiment.

The Love we are trying to describe is, through Itself, Uniqueness, a divine quality, in permanent connection with unconditional Beauty, Kindness and Love. Its living expression does not ask for or demand anything in exchange, from anyone. It only exists, as a state, holy and hallowing, through Itself.

Simply learning information about Love is of no help to us. True understanding appears only when we experience It, in a real way, by melting with It – a state of happiness – revealing, by Itself, Its universal grandeur and greatness.

By using the path of "Self-knowing", all is revealed to us without doing anything in particular. Simply becoming conscious of the reactions of the mind to the permanent challenges of Life in Its unfoldment makes them spontaneously disappear. In the "void" or "psychological emptiness" thus created, the whole being becomes united (body, mind and Spirit as "One"). In this short flash, experienced as all-encompassing peace, the individual encounters his Real Nature – as part of Godliness, which is, in fact, Love.

Therefore, the essence of our being is Love, that is, God as creative action, operating beneficial transformations. As soon as we discover this priceless Treasure, we will see everything through the eyes of God; not only our fellow beings but also all that exists in the Immense Universe.

Life

Life is breath and movement – a permanent communion,
Perpetual transformation. The old form, through cause
                                        and effect,
Born from an initial tendency – as a natural movement,
Through constant impulses, it changes into more evolved
                                        forms.

Wherever you look, All is Alive, there is Life in
                                        Everything,
A leaf of grass, an insect, a human being. Even so-called
                                        still life
Is a wise movement, for its Essence is the same.
Everywhere in the Universe, there is One Energy,
It is in fact Eternity, in perfect harmony.

When encountering Life, the wise man takes everything
                                        as it comes,
A true comprehension of the all-encompassing Truth;
Facts do not create any problems, if encountered
                                        correctly,
It is just a game of cause-effect, searching for fulfillment.

Death is a new beginning, a leap into a new dimension,
One form dissipates, but its Essence remains,
Aspiring to evolution, through non-action.
We need to give all our Attention to the Alive, to the
Aliveness,
Free of blind delusions – we find the true meaning.

Life is Energy – fueling Itself through Itself – in eternal movement and perpetual transformation. The old melting with the new create evolutionary impulses, manifested in newer and more evolved forms.

Wherever we look, everything we see contains within the Essence of the Aliveness in its continuous mobility. Therefore, Life is present in all that exists: a grain of sand, a leaf of grass, an insect, a human being. Within the Boundless, diverse in all its forms of manifestation, there is only one Energy, which we can describe as Divinity.

What is our attitude, as human beings, when we encounter the greatness of existence? The wise man can only have a humble attitude towards Life, filled with awe and respect. He welcomes all phenomena, events and happenings as they are, brought forth by the flow of Life. The simplicity of this encounter does not create any problems, if performed in the correct manner.

In fact, all the events and trials we encounter during our lifetime are determined by the Universal Law of Cause and Effect. Pleasant as well as painful effects are natural consequences of all the causes that we ourselves created in the past. By correctly encountering these effects, they are spontaneously dissolved and, with their disappearance, the causal energies are also dissipated.

In order to perfectly understand Life in Its universal unfoldment, we need to encounter It with the flame of

Attention. With the help of lucid, all-encompassing Attention we attain the peace of the soul or the psychological death of the past recorded as a memory. Simultaneously, without any intervention on our part, we experience a new beginning, as a factor of spiritual progress.

Therefore the Aliveness – pure immortal Essence, existent within us as well as everywhere in existence – needs to be approached with respect, by understanding the false and the ephemeral.

Clarity

It has no limits and no bounds, an immense living light,
Beyond any images – a harmonious whole.
In this clarity, thinking is completely still;
In a state of duality, it oscillates day and night.

The whole being is silent, absorbed in clarity,
Of infinite proportions, it is, in fact, unity.
It is a shadowless light, moving forward only,
Nothing can stop its hallowing impulses.

When thinking tries to grasp it, it becomes darkness,
You cannot cultivate it, for any such attempts are futile;
It is detached from thinking and from any imagination,
Through itself Reality, beyond any thoughts.

We encounter it naturally, when we see – spontaneously –
How thinking ruminates reality, mixing life with
                                    imagination.
In such an encounter, the human being is a light unto
                                    himself,
Darkness disappears without any trace.

Extended into clarity, free from desires,
The human being is Kindness, Love and Wisdom.
Attention is our support in this encounter,
Through it, the Sacred manifests Itself as infinite Love.

The clarity or lucidity of the mind we are trying to describe
in this poem is a state we can attain, as human beings, in
moments of high spiritual experience. In that very moment,
we function – body and mind as one unity – in perfect
harmony. The absence of any thinking activity inevitably
transports us into a state of superconsciousness, melting us
into the Cosmic Consciousness.

In this state, we exist outside time and space, as an
indivisible whole, perceived as indestructible light and
harmony. We are the invulnerable "Whole" itself. Any
feeling of separation is absent. The duality characteristic of
the ordinary mind has been eliminated simultaneously
with the disappearance of the "ego".

Functioning as a boundless unity, melting into

Universality, we move only in the present. We have a new mind, pure and uncontaminated by any previous recordings. In the flow of such a mind, the quality of holiness is revealed to us.

This mind is felt and expressed as: Love, Beauty and a limitless Joy; they are unlike anything we experience in the climate of the "ego".

The moment the chaotic, limited thinking intervenes in any shape or form, the wonder of boundlessness disappears. We return to the limited world, ruled by ignorance and darkness, and our whole existence is engulfed in conflictual states, fear and sorrow.

How can we encounter this wondrous clarity?

From the very beginning, a point needs to be made. The clarity we mention here is not a goal to be reached, something that the mind can imagine and, through effort and will, performed in time, can one day attain. In such attempts, both the projection of clarity and the pursuit of clarity as an act of will are elements of disharmony, through their very nature, specific to the activity of the "ego", strictly connected to the finite world. Each such accomplishment takes place within the same dimension and can only fortify its limitedness.

Therefore, clarity can never be attained through the activity of the mind, no matter how knowledgeable or well intentioned it might be. The simple desire is, by its very nature, a state of disturbance, creating even more confusion and disorder.

If we realize – in a real way, not just intellectually – that disorder and confusion are the cause of the problem, which needs to be solved immediately, instead of pursuing clarity – in that moment, the thinking process, exposed as the perturbing factor, becomes silent. It is an effortless silence, not wanted, forced or imagined in any way. The simple act of exposing it makes it become quiet.

In that moment of surprise and silence, clarity projects its light as a state of lucid Attention. It is the Sacred itself within the depth of our being, showering its blessings on us. Therefore, this clarity is attained indirectly, by simply becoming conscious of the disorder initiated and maintained by the activity of "ego". To put it another way: silence has given the Divine Spark the opportunity to shower its light on us, demonstrating our divine origin and our immense potential.

I would like to end this explanation by inviting you to read each verse one more time; in its clear expression, in simple words, it invites you to discover this reality for yourselves, through a direct experience. Do not simply read the poem without experiencing this phenomenon, mobilizing the whole capacity of the Sacred within, defining you as a complete being.

Being and experiencing as many moments of "lucid Attention" represents the key to success, uniting you with the Great Light from which all and everything originates.

Joy

A spring of alive water, with its source in the Limitless,
Priceless climate of delight, touched only by the Sacred,
Untouched by the influence from the outside or the
                              impulses coming from within,
When the ephemeral disappears.

It is a divine music, a harmony in itself,
Within the rhythm of the Universe, synchronized as
                                      a whole;
Joy is the essence of life, empowering the individual,
When the union is total, the being is pure movement.

In this Oneness, the being expands into Infinity,
Beyond the limited. The "self" is excluded
And its state of fragmentation – always confined
In its purpose and motivations – a slave of time.

Joy is not an explosive state of enthusiasm or pleasure,
It is not an emotional state based on comfort;
It is not connected to thought or fictitious desires,
These are ordinary expectations, created by time.

It cannot be desired or cultivated as a flower,
Imagined as an idea or sought passionately;
Joy is completely independent, detached from thought,
A self-consuming boundless flame.

It appears spontaneously, when limitless silence
Envelops us, integrating everything;
Joy rejoices all within us and around us,
Man becomes kind and tolerant, for he is boundless.

Joy is a strange phenomenon; the mind of the ordinary
man, conditioned by the residues of time, cannot
comprehend it. It has no connection with any emotional
states achieved as a result of a success, whether it be
physical or intellectual. Therefore, Joy cannot be obtained,
achieved or cultivated, in any manner or form.

It appears spontaneously, beyond the dominion of will,
when the "ego" disappears and the practitioner is united
with Boundlessness. In a state of equilibrium and perfect
harmony, the blissful individual is united with the
Universal Harmony; thus he experiences and comprehends
– firsthand – the state of joy or happiness.

What else can we say about Joy – naturally, only after we
have encountered it from our own experience and not from
other people's descriptions of it?

Joy does not manifest itself in an explosive, enthusiasm-
like manner. Similarly, it is not connected to the senses, as
is the case with pleasure and satisfaction.

When Joy is present, the structure of the limited man,
conditioned by time, has completely disappeared. Whoever
has enjoyed a beautiful sunset has truly experienced the joy
of melting with nature. In that moment of intense

experience, the thinking "self" spontaneously melts into the simplicity of the encounter with the beauty of the natural phenomenon.

When Joy is truly experienced, it has beneficial effects on the entire human attitude. Understanding, tolerance and kindness overflow, as a heavenly nectar, onto our surrounding environment – and not only.

In fact, the individual, living in the moment, in perfect union with Divinity, becomes a true creator. Through his living experience, he creates a different world, in which Love proves that the "state of paradise" is not a mere fiction. It can be realized here, on Earth, through our day-to-day, moment-to-moment constant diligence. "Self-knowing" is available to you; it is something that can be truly experienced. Its effectiveness is reflected in its immediate results, if applied in the right manner.

Physical Relaxation

Physical relaxation is attained through silence,
An absolute silence, without efforts or will;
Simply becoming aware of what makes us tense
                                and nervous
Creates perfect harmony.

Energy accumulates within us and it makes us whole,
Only in this manner can we experience the oneness of
being;
When the "ego" perishes, the "psychological void" ensues
As a blessing, expanding into Eternity.

In this state, we transcend our nature,
"One" with Infinity – as perfection.
A new Man is born and, through him, a new world
is created,
For the individual and the world are closely connected.

Both disease and health are created by the mind,
Therefore we need to be aware of it each moment;
Attention creates a climate of beneficial peace,
It is the Flame that burns everything we like or dislike.

The Purity of the Energy – a state of divinity –
Reveals itself in this context, as a true Reality.
We all have the potential to experience it, to live as total
relaxation,
It cannot be attained through desire or force, or any ideal
formulas.

Relaxation is a state of calmness or lack of tension; it is
accomplished without any need for acts of will, effort or
struggle – when thinking is completely silent.

With the help of lucid Attention, we simply come into
direct contact with the activity of the mind, which is the
root cause of any states of turmoil. The simplicity of this

encounter makes it become spontaneously silent, without any other intervention on our part.

As thinking disappears, harmony and the holy peace of the soul ensue, without desiring or pursuing it. In that moment we have an immense energy and, as a whole being, we live in timelessness. As the "ego" disappears into the "psychological void" ensuing naturally, we directly experience the state of universality.

In this fortunate circumstance – detached from the ancestral mind – we are a new Man; through our simple act of living this reality, we create a different world in which creative Love leads us.

In present days, scientists have come to the conclusion that the majority of diseases are caused by psychological stress. And the "ego" or the "personal self" is guilty of creating this constant state of turmoil. We have no other solution but to dissipate its whole structure, as well as its fragmentary energies, which support and initiate its fictitious existence. In order to demolish it, the only instrument we need is an impersonal all-encompassing Attention – we encounter the "ego" in the moment, as it appears in the form of mental reactions.

Practically, Attention is like a flame, burning and pulverizing both pleasant and painful impressions. With their disappearance, in the "psychological void" that ensues, we encounter an Immense Energy as a state of Pure Consciousness – a state of timeless "being". In this circumstance, the relaxation of the whole body occurs naturally; all human beings can attain this state – without resorting to will, desire or imagination as a goal to fulfill.

Understanding

A product of clarity, revealing the hidden meaning
of things,
Opening horizons towards Truth or falsehoods.
When understanding is not present, life is a haze,
Relationship is a fiction and action is chaotic.

According to depth, there are three layers
of understanding:
Superficial understanding – at the level of words;
Mental understanding, an association of concepts;
And finally, total understanding – which is boundless.

Total understanding is – by itself and through itself –
true understanding,
Its spontaneous perception breaks the sphere of
the limited,
The chains of the mind are shattered, in a state
of freedom,
All is enlightened in the sparkle of clarity.

Attention is the key, providing comprehension,
Through it, all is clear and we grasp the essence of things
spontaneously,
Being and action – the beginning of transformation,
It dispels the darkness of the mind through full
Enlightenment.

Through spontaneous understanding, we are an
integral being,
Melting with life, each moment is true within us.
We are one with Immensity, in syntony with the rhythm
of the Universe,
Through it, the fragmentation is dissolved.

Truth, Love, Kindness and Wisdom are revealed,
As a gift of freedom and divine fulfillment.
We can reach it through silence and a humble attitude,
The past disappears instantly and there is no future.

Understanding appears as a result of inner harmony and
mental clarity, in the light of lucid Attention. With the help
of Attention, facts are understood and perceived in their
clarity, either as truths, or as evident and undeniable falsehoods. This understanding cannot be interpreted or
denied.

There are also two other levels of understanding. The
first, a basic understanding, which takes place at the level
of words. The second one, intellectual or associative understanding, based on the memories of the "ego". It is relative
and in close connection with its source; the "self" initiates
it, sustains it and tries to prove its reality.

We are interested in total understanding, demonstrating its truth through itself, by itself. Only at this level of understanding will there be a unanimous consensus in the interpretation of facts, events etc.

This understanding appears spontaneously, when the "ego" ceases its activity. Attention is the miraculous key, ensuring the success of the experience. Here is how: the ordinary man, with his subjective-selfish mind, functioning through mechanical reactions, is incapable of correctly encountering and understanding life. Any attempts in this regard inevitably result in contradictions, conflicts and tensional states. The newness of the aliveness cannot fit into the old patterns of thought.

As we become aware of this incompatibility between the old and the new, the mind becomes silent, unconditionally. Seeing its total powerlessness, it becomes humble, through silence.

This revelation is indestructibly connected to the flash of Attention. Or, to put it in a better way, Attention opened – through the dark climate of the conditioned mind – a path of light coming from and towards the Infinite.

Therefore, we can experience Truth, Love, Wisdom only in the humble silence of the conditioned mind, when all that has been accumulated disappears suddenly and there are no projections into the future.

When experiencing this state – as we have described it – let us remember that the phenomenon of liberation from the domination of the "ego" starts with liberation itself. We are free from the first moment – in the humble silence of thinking – we are also free as the moment is consumed; we welcome the next moment in the same manner, and so on.

Doubt everything, so you can discover for yourself the falsehood of all theories which describe Liberation as an ideal to accomplish sometime in the future. Such endeavor is a pointless waste of time and energy.

In fact, all paths towards so-called spiritual fulfillment which follow a certain theory only result in deceit, and they further fortify the stronghold of the "ego", isolating us from the authentic moment of liberation.

Life after the So-Called Death

Human beings are afraid and constantly anxious of death,
Yet it is nothing but a frightening mirage, proving
That the individual, as an incarnated being, is ignorant,
Considering his body to be his true being.

Yet the body is not the being, only a planetary piece
$\qquad\qquad\qquad\qquad\qquad\qquad$ of clothing,
Destined to disappear, when it becomes damaged;
Whereas Life, through Itself and by Itself, as vital Energy,
Will never die, for It is a timeless inexhaustible Source.

This vital Force dwelling in man, as well as in animals,
Is a bundle of thoughts and emotional states,
Called personality, or the psychological layer,
Or the Soul – pervading the physical body.

It provides the body with strength, existence and value,
No one can destroy it, for it lives eternally;
When the body is no longer able to fulfill its purpose,
The Soul withdraws – Spirit guides his departure.

After you've left the body, all is peaceful, quiet,
Pain, suffering, instincts instantly disappear,
Death is like a swoon – all bodily sensations disappear:
Fear, thirst, phobias and mental anxieties.

When the Soul is called outside of the body,
It rises to the crown chakra – the pituitary gland;
As it exits the body, it becomes a free Soul,
The body immediately dies – extinguished in a flash.

The whole process lasts an instant and it is painless,
In the moment of liberation from dense matter,
                    a transformation occurs:
We reach a new plane – an existence of Light,
Where we are only Spirit and absolute emotion.

Our body is Light, a mirror of our thought frequency,
Accepted by that form of Light, our own being;
Starting from here, we visit the seven skies,
According to our thoughts and emotional attitudes.

The sky we reach is based on the life we have lived;
                              there are seven levels.
The first level is the physical plane, with successes
                                    and failures;
When we leave the body, we will be attracted to
                              a similar plane
According to the level of vibration of our consciousness
                        and our present understanding.

The heritage we take from our life on Earth
Will be reflected in our way of life; it is the currency
By which we access skies of fear and suffering,
Or skies of certain powers and Love as a living
                                    experience.

Divinity is seen in all the planes; It is Life, in Its
                              eternal presence.
Let us always remember that It is Life itself.
Any thought we consider or pursue
Has a certain vibration or frequency.

We experience all this permanently, as feelings;
When we oppose pain, we create thoughts of
                        a similar resonance,
Which increase the pain through their limitedness,
In their essence, these thoughts emanate gross vibrations.

When Love intervenes, as understanding and expression,
A field of higher vibrations is created.
The sky we will go to is a reflection of our consciousness.
Our spirit is attracted by corresponding vibes.

Therefore, our Life on Earth, as well as after
                                   the so-called death
Is absolutely connected to thoughts, reflected in
                                   consciousness.
Let us explain how Life unfolds
On the seven planes of existence:

The first plane is the physical, connected to
                              the carnal body,
God is understood on this material plane,
Revealed by an awake consciousness and by mastering
The reactions of the mind and its deceitful imagination.

All the other planes are connected to the physical,
                              a constant integration,
Here, Divinity reveals itself as the witness,
As boundless, unconditional Love,
We live, in a real way, as One with God.

The second plane is the astral – a separate dimension
Of more refined matter and different laws of action.
After we leave the body – Spirit and Soul as one,
Here, we relive the past of our previous existence;

The film of our previous life is played,
With pain, remorse, self-blame – according to our
                                                    behavior.
We learn from its effects, pursuing our divine perfection.
Climbing step by step, unfolding the potential of the Self.

The third plane is the mental – on an inferior level
It is connected to personal power,
A desire to dominate our fellow beings, through slavery,
Possession, pride, hypocrisy – its constant companions.

In this dimension, the only reality is personal conviction,
Forcing another to say what you believe;
Your own point of view is nothing but a repetition,
Meaningless and worthless.

The fourth plane, a superior mental plane,
The known is the master, it mesmerizes us;
We know about Light, Love, but only in words,
Without expressing it towards All and Everything.

Self-importance, hypocrisy and their masks
Dwell in this climate and its false realization;
Great words are being uttered,
Devoid of any real experience.

The fifth plane, the causal, is manifest as a paradise,
Here, all is Light, a wonderful dream-like climate,
Any thought is fulfilled, as endless Love,
Harmony and beauty are encountered everywhere;

Never-before-seen palaces, suspended gardens,
A divine music in perfect harmony with all.
When souls reach here, they are mesmerized by
                                     this climate,
They forget about their destiny, for long periods of time.

Everything is instantly fulfilled, without will or
                                     expectation,
They dwell here for thousands of years, overwhelmed
                                     by abundance.
Nevertheless, at one point, they must ask the question:
Where does the Light originate from, as well as the music
                                     and fullness?

Finally, they realize that the wondrous Energy,
Existent everywhere, in perfect harmony,
Is the manifest flow of Life, pervading All,
Nothing is separate from Its Great complexity.

When these fortunate beings know this, through their
                                     sacred Love,
They understand It and express It, from their living
                                     experience.
From now on, they see Oneness in living beings and things,
Ready to experience superior levels.

The sixth plane is called the spiritual sky,
There is Oneness with essence,
Oneness with All Life – it is an open gate
To the next level – as a precise fulfillment.

For all that man perceives, manifested as Real,
He intuitively knows it is Real, in a certain and true way,
He becomes "One" with the Real;
This is the law and its natural effect.

Finally, the seventh plane, a Sublime Spiritual Sky.
Here, all is brightness – a surreal climate,
A Unique Source of Light – an expanding Ocean
Of hallowing Energies as eternal freshness.

From the Heart of Light, emanating Light,
Man as a divine being emerges,
Meditating-contemplating on the Sacred brightness,
He becomes that which he contemplates.

All human beings are destined to reach this Sky,
And experience it as understanding and Wisdom,
Living and unfolding their Life's potential;
We have all we need within us.

On the threshold of this Sky, Trinity becomes whole,
Body, mind and Spirit are One, united with Divinity,
United with our fellow beings, united with All;
Direct Knowing guides our steps, moment to moment.

The phenomenon of death creates so much fear, anguish and terror for human beings; yet it is nothing but a frightening mirage, demonstrating the incarnated beings' lack of understanding, by considering the physical body to be the only reality.

The body is a mere piece of clothing that we put on in order to experience the material world. When this garment has deteriorated, we – the real being – abandon it and continue our existence in other dimensions.

We, the real being, are Vital Energy, a Spark in the Immense Divine Flame, which will never die, for we have similar qualities with the Creative Divine. This Vital Force is a bundle of thoughts and emotional states, creating our individuality, which permeates the physical body; it is also called Soul or the psychological layer.

This Spark – the true Man – gives vitality and value to the physical body throughout its existence on this planet. When the physical body is unable to fulfill its role as a host, the Soul withdraws from this temporary abode, following the guidance of Spirit.

As we leave the body, everything becomes peaceful and quiet. All our worries, needs, suffering and fears disappear. Death is similar to a swoon; hunger, thirst as well as mental anxieties vanish. When the Soul is called outside of the body – as we have shown earlier – he rises towards the crown of the head, to the pituitary gland and, as soon as he leaves the body, he becomes a free Soul. Devoid of Vital Energy, the body is immediately extinguished and dies. The whole process takes place in a second and it is painless.

The moment we become free from our earthly garment, a radical change occurs. We reach a new plane, a plane of Light; as Soul and Spirit, we function in a body of light – an exact replica of the carnal body we have just deserted. This is our astral body, the double of our physical structure, made up of infinite particles of Light.

Starting from this level, we will rise towards the seven levels of consciousness or seven skies, according to our thoughts and emotional attitudes. The skies vary according to how Life is lived on each level of existence.

Let us start from the first level, the physical, experienced as successes and failures. The moment we leave this plane, as we detach from our physical body, we will be attracted – just like a strong magnet – towards a level of vibration similar to our knowledge and memory heritage when we left the Earth. These qualities will determine our level of existence in that dimension; they are our currency. On that plane, we will suffer or rejoice, according to the qualities we have stored during our previous Life on Earth.

In this context, let us remember that God is Life Itself, in Its eternal presence. Each thought we put out has a certain vibration or distinct frequency that we experience as emotions or feelings. When we oppose pain, for instance, we create similar thoughts, which amplify the already existent pain, for they have a dense vibration. If, on the contrary, we intervene with Love, as well as understanding and expression, we will give out a different type of vibration, of a finer, superior quality.

The sky we will go to is strictly connected to the quality of our consciousness. The Spirit, with His layers, is attracted to similar vibrations, thanks to the qualities He is endowed with. Therefore, the quality of our Life here on Earth, as well as after the so-called death, is strictly connected to our thinking, reflecting itself in our individual consciousness.

Let us see how Life unfolds on the seven planes or levels of existence.

The first plane is the physical, tied to the carnal body. On this level of existence, God can be truly understood and perceived by an awake Consciousness and a total mastery of the reactions of the mind, which is dominated by imagination. On this level we can experience all seven planes, when our being is Integrated. On this plane, God manifests Itself as boundless and unconditional Love, and we live, in a real way, as "One" with God.

The second plane or the astral is a separate dimension. It is created out of finer matter, with different laws and manner of action. After we leave the physical body – Spirit and Soul together as one, as a body made of astral matter, we will relive – as if in a movie – our previous existence. We will remember pain, remorse and regrets, according to our behavior in that life. In this manner, from the effects of this remembrance, we learn not to repeat the same mistakes and to pursue our spiritual perfection.

The third plane, called the inferior mental plane, has the characteristic of power, an inner desire to dominate our fellow beings, through possession and slavery; arrogance and hypocrisy are our constant companions. In this dimension, personal conviction is the only reality, the desire to force another being to believe and declare what we want them to. And our point of view is nothing but a meaningless and pointless permanent repetition of the old.

On the fourth level, the superior mental plane, knowledge affirms itself and mesmerizes us. Here, we know what Light is and what Holy Love is, without being able to express it towards All and Everything. Such knowledge is limited to the level of words, devoid of any real experience. Self-praise, hypocrisy and deceitful masks find a favorable climate here and create a false sense of realization. Words are being uttered, without any reality behind them. Such arrogant affirmations are devoid of any feeling and experience.

The fifth level, or the causal plane, is defined as

paradise. Here, all is Light, a true climate of splendor as well as dream and imagination. Any thought is instantly fulfilled as endless Love. Harmony and Beauty reign everywhere. Never-before-seen palaces, suspended gardens, as well as divine music in perfect harmony with the whole ambiance. When the Soul reaches this plane, mesmerized by this climate, he forgets his destiny for very long periods of time, as all his desires are immediately fulfilled. Abundance and over-satisfaction – a true ideal temptation – overwhelm the Soul.

Nevertheless, at some point, one must ask the obvious question: Where does this Light, delightful music and overwhelming abundance come from? A permanent flow of Life, permeating All and Everything; nothing within this Immense complexity is separated! When the fortunate experiencer realizes this, through Love, he understands his destiny and now he is ready to ascend to higher levels of consciousness. He returns to Earth, interested in a different kind of experience. Detached from abundance, he constantly pursues real Happiness, in Union with the Divine and Its Eternal Realm, as well as boundless Love, as the only goal towards realization.

The sixth plane, called the spiritual Sky, is an open gate towards the next level, as a precise fulfillment. For all that man perceives as Real, unfolding before him, he knows it is Real, in a certain and undeniable way, and he becomes the Real, as an Integrated Man. This is, in fact, the law of realization, perfecting itself through itself, as an unavoidable fact.

The final plane, the seventh, is implicitly experienced as a Sublime Spiritual Sky. Here, all is brightness, a surreal climate, as a Unique Source of Light, an Immense expanding Ocean of hallowing Energies, as eternal freshness. And from the Heart of Light, emanating Light, someone appears, a Human Being – Divine Creature – meditating and contemplating on that Sacred Brightness. He becomes that which he contemplates.

This Sky is the destiny of every human being living on this Earth. We can attain it through understanding and Wisdom, and we can realize it through that particular emotion and vibration. We have all the necessary qualities in order to experience and explore this grand potential of Life successfully. On the threshold of this Sky – in the face of Eternity – this is what we need to fulfill practically: the Unity of our being – body, mind and Spirit, together as One. As a functional Whole, we are One with the Creative Divine, in perfect Communion. In this simple state of "Being" or Pure Consciousness, the gate to Eternity opens in front of us and we discover, through a real experience, boundless Love towards our fellow beings, as well as towards the Whole Existence.

Listening to Noise

Noise is a mixture of dissonant sounds, of various intensities; it can eventually reach maximum levels of vibration, with destructive effects, able to damage our auditory organ, leading to hearing loss. Let us remind of a few examples of noise, which our daily Life provides abundantly: the noise of a car, a dog barking, a baby's cry, a door squeaking, the whistle of a siren, the sound of a trumpet, a train moving, a thunderstorm, the clamor of a sports stadium, an airplane etc.

All of these noises have a particular impact on the human psyche, especially when they occur unexpectedly.

A different kind of noise – more subtle – comes from our inner world; it is the noise of thoughts, overflowing and arising from the reactions of the mind, as it encounters any Life phenomenon. These thoughts isolate us from the Reality of the present moment and force us to relive – in our imagination – facts and events we once experienced in a distant past and preserved in the memory as images. By selecting images from the same past, we project ourselves into an uncertain and irrelevant imaginary future. In both cases, we are and we manifest ourselves like string puppets, maneuvered by the fictitious "ego" or the mind conditioned by time-space.

Whether noises come from the external world or from the inner world, in both circumstances we are practically faced with a challenge, representing a wonderful opportunity to realize the Oneness of our being.

If we function as "egos", that is, as a fragment in which the mind judges and analyzes according to its contradictory values: pleasant or unpleasant – in that case the noise disturbs and troubles us, and our whole being loses contact with Reality. Furthermore, this psychological unrest has dramatic effects on the health of our physical body. Sadness, sorrow, stress and, finally, disease and premature death are the negative effects of our erroneous way of functioning at the level of the "personal self".

In "Self-knowing", when we experience the Wholeness of our being, Love leads us through Its own Reality. In this fortunate circumstance, any noises are welcomed and accepted as they come. The simplicity of this encounter, as a complete Man, leads to the disappearance of their importance.

Let us try this experiment from a different angle. Noise is a wonderful opportunity to realize the Oneness of being, when body, mind and Spirit are united as a whole, in order to embrace the disturbing phenomenon.

In conclusion, let us bless any noises, as well as any surprises that Life brings us in Its movement, for they are wonderful opportunities to know ourselves: both as a fictitious entity, as well as Real Divine Nature, That Which We Truly Are – true Love and true Godliness.

The Aliveness

The Aliveness, Pure Energy, existent in everyone
        and everything in the immense Universe,
It is Truth, Light, Love, Intelligence and perfect Beauty.
The Source that created It has no beginning, no end,
Only "It Exists", beyond time and space.

It created everything that exists in the Universe,
In Its indescribable Kindness and Wisdom.
If you are confused, deeming these words as empty,
        lacking in content,
Let us investigate the mysterious Aliveness together.

We don't start this journey with a mind full of opinions
        or theories,
For it would become an obstacle, such deceit prevents
        the investigation;
Therefore we set off
Totally relaxed and free from what we have accumulated
        throughout time.
We eliminate the past, through all-encompassing
        Attention, focalized in the present,
Encountering images and thoughts
Arising from the ancestral past and memory.

The mind – an empty vessel – free from time, therefore
                              completely independent,
Is able to encompass the newness of Life – eternally new,
                              never repeating itself.
Traveling together, each for himself, here is what we
                              accomplish.
Let us continue.

The Aliveness, existent within us, appears only in one
                              circumstance,
When we do not want it, do not imagine it, do not call for it,
When the psychological past recorded in the mind
                              completely vanishes.
This psychological death is essential.
Let thoughts, knowledge and attachments disappear,
As well as the knower, the entity who knows
                              or experiences.

There is nothing left of the "ego", only a lucid Attention,
                              a state of Enlightenment.
Thus, the Aliveness reveals itself to us, in this very life,
                              enveloping us completely.
When we die physically, we only melt with this Aliveness,
Detached from everything that tied us to life,
Various bondages: to persons, things, fame, glory or ideas
                              that bind us.

Is it easy? Difficult? Do you understand what I have just
         described
From direct personal experience, or just intellectually?
When the mind only understands words connected
        grammatically,
What the author describes has not been understood!
Try again, re-read, remain alone with yourself, as one
         movement;

It is just a clear, simple and direct experience,
The entity who tries to know, accumulate and understand
       the unknowable is totally excluded.
The merit is solely yours, through a real experience,
Any teacher is excluded. Try to understand the meaning
Of what the verse merely points to.

The Aliveness is Pure Energy; It encompasses and
permeates all that exists, in the entire Universe, seen or
unseen. It is: Truth, Beauty, Love, Intelligence and perfect
Harmony. It has no beginning and no end. In fact, only the
Aliveness exists, by Itself and through Itself, and in Its
immense Kindness It has created everything within the
great Infinite. These affirmations are not empty words –
mere mechanical repetitions – such as the ones uttered by
knowing, repetitive and obsessive minds.

If you find these statements confusing, dear friend, I
invite you to come with me and, together, let us try to
investigate this mysterious Aliveness. In this exploration,
we do not need any opinions, faiths or theories, for they
are mere obstacles obstructing our journey, creating
illusions.

Therefore, let us start our journey completely relaxed, in

silence, free from all the burdens accumulated throughout time and preserved in the memory. We eliminate the past with the light of all-encompassing Attention, by focalizing it – in the present moment – on the bundle of images, feelings or mental reactions arising from the memorial past.

Therefore, the mind – an empty vessel, totally independent – is able to embrace the newness of Life manifested as perpetual freshness. Journeying together – but each conscious of himself – this is what we discover.

The Aliveness existent within us reveals Itself not through desire, wish or imagination, but only when the psychological past recorded by the mind vanishes completely. This psychological death is absolutely essential. Thoughts, knowledge, various attachments, as well as the knower, the entity who experiences – all disappear.

There is nothing left of the "ego". We are and will always be only a lucid all-encompassing Attention – a state of Enlightenment. Thus, the eternal Aliveness is revealed, in this life, in this body. When we die biologically, we will leave with this Aliveness, detaching from all attachments, such as people, possessions, glory, fame, faiths or ideals.

Is it difficult? Is it easy? How do you feel about all this? Do you understand it from direct experience, or are you confined to superficial intellectual understanding? If your mind has only understood the words and their grammatical sense, in that case you have not understood what the author conveyed. Try again, re-read, remain alone with yourself as a united being, in direct contact with the reality of the moment. In fact, it is a simple, clear and direct experience. The knower – the entity that knows, accumulates and tries to understand that which cannot be understood – is completely excluded.

The whole merit is yours – as an authentic, direct

experience – in which the experiencer, the creator of duality, has vanished.

You also need to completely eliminate and ignore the author, the person who wrote this book. This is what I am continuously trying to explain in poems and prose, so you can better grasp "Self-knowing". It all depends on you and you alone. Your persistent work and inner honesty will provide you from the very beginning with clear signs, proving the efficiency of this message.

Aloneness

Totally emptying the mind of its whole content,
The being is completely detached from the old past.
A priceless climate of freedom, a natural leap into
                                        Boundlessness,
Life as Oneness – man expanding into Infinity.

Thinking cannot accept it, the mind is always fearful,
In its arrogance, it does not want to lose what it possesses;
It accumulates what it likes, wants, desires or prefers,
Accumulating is its nature and its treasure.

When any trace of fear disappears, the mind is
                              completely empty,
Effortlessly, the being becomes whole,
The energy accumulates, body and mind are a unity,
Truth – Reality interwoven.

The empty mind is like an empty drum, resonating
When it is hit, it vibrates like a string;
It is beyond the dimension of time; through silence,
                              it is action,
Being "one" with the Universe – it becomes Wisdom.

When aloneness is present in the depth of our being,
We will know Beauty and Kindness, from direct
                              experience.
Nothing affects us and we don't accumulate anything,
Universal in the moment, we are integrated into the
                              "Whole".

Aloneness appears when we watch the movement
Of fear, hatred, personal agendas, success and frustration,
Or when we encompass desire, in permanent turmoil,
Always fighting other desires for supremacy.

If we encounter all with an all-encompassing Attention,
It dissipates and shatters any ideal forms;
Through it, the Sacred envelops us, renewing and
                              healing us,
Man becomes Love – perpetually creative.

The phenomenon of aloneness, experienced in moments of existence, represents the beginning and end of "Self-knowing".

Practically, it is realized by totally emptying the mind of its whole content, recorded in the memory. In that moment, the individual, free from his whole past, attains the full functioning potential of his being and is integrated into Infinity.

The mind of the ordinary man, centered on egoistic values, in which pleasure and vanity play an important part, rejects aloneness, deeming it to be the enemy of its existence. How could it renounce the treasure of knowledge, for through it, it defines itself as wise, by feeding on pleasant memories, flattering the self-image of the deceptive "self"!

What can we do about such a mind, filled with arrogance, afraid of disappearing into nothingness? Can we distinguish its reality, existent in our way of being and of manifesting ourselves?

Discovering what is happening within our being requires a lot of honesty on our part!

If we are aware of this reality, as mind sees for itself its erroneous way of functioning, it becomes silent, in humbleness. In that moment of non-activity, our being becomes whole. Body and mind are a single unit, a pure energy in which Truth-Reality is revealed.

In order to better understand this phenomenon, let us use a simile. When the mind is empty, as we described earlier, it is like an empty drum, vibrating only when something touches it. The rest of the time, it remains inactive – or silent; in this silence, action takes place, as a beneficial Transformative Reality. Through silence, the individual mind encounters the Universal Mind and is integrated into it, in a perfect way.

Therefore, when aloneness envelops our being totally, we will know, from personal experience, what Love, Beauty and Truth are, on an absolute level.

Before ending, let us explain the simplicity of practicing "Self-knowing".

We cannot reach aloneness as an ideal to pursue and fulfill, through desire, efforts of will, imagination etc. All these means of accomplishment belong to the "ego", and they cannot transcend the limits which define them.

Aloneness envelops us spontaneously, when we come into contact with what Aloneness is not, that is, through an encounter with "what is", "what appears" on the screen of our consciousness, such as fears, goals, successes, frustrations, ambitions, arrogance, hatred etc. We also become aware of the constant struggle taking place between various desires, each aspiring to supremacy.

All of these are encountered in simplicity, with the flame of Attention; they are dissipated, without leaving any trace. In the empty space that ensues, the Sacred within every human being reveals Itself as Love, creating a new man and, through him, creating a new world, with a different mentality from the one we live in at the moment.

The Voice Within

This voice, coming from the depths of our being,
Does not originate in the "ego", in the narrow
                                   closed mind,
Limited to the past, conditioned by time,
Never capable of a real encounter.

Its source is beyond time – in the immense purity,
Never repeating itself, always newness;
The voice does not cheat or lie, it guides us with wisdom,
Ready to assist us at any time, whenever we request it.

The humble mind must be silent – an absolute silence,
There are no expectations or imaginary goals;
In this psychological void, the purity within us ensues
As Love, Beauty and Truth in movement.

The present moment unites us with Infinity,
And with all there is – as a complete man.
No conflicts or turmoil, no mistakes or sins,
Can exist in this climate.

Always seek advice from the depths, by asking a simple
question:
What should I do? How to solve this? Followed by
silence...
This simplicity gives answers from its immense clarity,
The mind just reaps them.

Often, its advice defies human logic,
It will probably make perfect sense sometime
in the future,
Follow it anyway, empty the vessel of consciousness,
For the fleeting and the limited are blind advisors.

The Infinite

We cannot experience it through our limitedness!
How can you ensnare Eternal Boundlessness in the cage
of the mind?
When the limited is silent, the Infinite envelops us,
Through it, our being expands into the Absolute.

Integrated into Infinity, we live true Love,
It disintegrates all conflictual states;
Eternal being – integrated into Infinity –
Reveals the beauty of life and its Sacred Reality.

Each individual has the potential
To experience the Infinite with his whole being;
Just watch and listen to the flow of life in eternal
                                        movement,
The simplicity of the encounter is the realization.

Thoughts, images, desires are watched wholly,
Light-Attention dissolves any duality;
This encounter transcends us into the Limitless,
Just being, beyond purpose, we expand into Infinity.

Spontaneity

The lightning of the moment, appearing and
                                disappearing,
An impulse in our life, dying in a flash...
Overflowing thoughts, images, desires, sensations
Torture our life – the "now" is misunderstood.

Existence is movement, measured through spontaneity,
If we don't embrace the moment, there is no
                        comprehension.
It is only by being really present that we perceive
                    the sparkle of the moment,
It requires wakefulness, diligence and perseverance.

Without it, we can never respond to the challenges of life,
In our ignorance, life becomes turmoil;
Man struggles like a bird caught in a net,
When he gives importance to the "self".

The struggle of the mind, seeking fulfillment,
Is a dull preoccupation, an empty fantasy!
We naturally become spontaneous when we are
                              lucid-attentive
To each movement of Life, mirrored in our consciousness.

Thoughts, emotions, faiths, born out of ignorance,
Or confused sentiments, fueled by desires,
Only a quiet mind is beyond conflict,
It does not analyze, nor does it pursue any models.

In absolute peace, the "ego" perishes,
Sensitive, lucid and still, we move eternally;
Encountering everything spontaneously,
We detach from what we have experienced,
Nothing is accumulated, no stories need to be told.

Living in this way – through a direct relationship,
We detach from the false and we discover the true path.
In this state, Love, Beauty and Kindness
Impose their Divine Law, in syntony with Reality.

Spontaneity, as a natural quality of the spirit, ensues instan-
taneously, by itself, able to embrace and comprehend the

eternal movement of the aliveness as newness and freshness from one moment to another.

The whole existence is a movement measured through this spontaneous flash, as something unexpected. In order to understand it, we need to have a sharp, alert mind, as well as determination, diligence and perseverance.

Therefore, any thought, image, desire, fear, ambition, as well as any sensation – if we do not watch them wholly and spontaneously the very moment they appear – eventually darken our life and create suffering.

The lack of spontaneity prevents us from giving an appropriate response to the countless challenges by which life tests us, according to the destiny that brought us to reincarnation on Earth.

A mind which desires to be spontaneous and makes efforts in this sense is an ignorant mind, directed by the confused and chained "ego"; by attempting to search for itself, the degradation of the "self" deepens.

We become naturally spontaneous when, using attention as light, we encounter everything that life brings in our path as an unconscious reflex. We encounter thoughts, emotions, faiths, fears etc. without turning this simple contact into a goal or ideal to accomplish.

Such a quiet mind does not lose itself in analyses, nor does it follow any patterns.

With this mind, the notions of "me" and "mine" disappear and we become sensitive, lucid and sponta-neous.

Everything we encounter, we come into contact with it, understand it and overcome it spontaneously; thus we are able to encounter the next moment in the same manner. Nothing is accumulated and nothing needs to be described. The Joy that this encounter bestows on us is a true blessing. It weakens the authority of time, which conditioned us.

By practicing this direct relationship, we detach from the false and we discover a new path, manifested as Love and beauty without cause. The mind, lucid in its purity, becomes an instrument of applying the Divine Law in moments of Reality.

Attention and the Sacred

The Sacred – the Source of Life – everywhere and
in everything, pervading all:
Galaxies, stars, planets and all their contents, sustained
by Love,
It was not created by anyone, It has always existed,
Without beginning, without end, It will always be,
eternally.

The Sacred is both stillness and movement,
It is not limited by anything, It is Infinity,
Affirming Itself as Kindness and boundless Love;
It does not force or coerce – Its patience is endless.

It does not impose Its law on human beings, It gives
                                        complete freedom,
In times of need, It helps us with the strict necessities.
We cannot encounter It with the limitedness of our mind,
For we merely reduce It to a false image of Its reality.

We can never encounter It through the "ego"
Or through the skill of the mind, trying to grasp It;
Comparing ourselves with It is a sacrilege,
For we only increase our self-importance.

"I Am" – only the Sacred can affirm it – the rest...
                                        all is fiction,
Without It, nothing lasts, any action is excluded;
In It, all is interwoven in a perfect harmony,
Only through It is the meaning of life revealed.

How can we encounter It, avoiding any deceit?
It is within us and within everyone, equally!
It affirms Itself spontaneously, when the mind is
                                        completely silent,
Silence opens Its gate – the whole being is newly born.

It is an unforced, unsought and unimagined silence,
A spontaneous realization. The individual mind can never
                                        attain it;
Will, effort, hope, mantras,
Prayers and beliefs are of no use.

Silence is attained in simplicity, clearly and consistently,
Through all-encompassing Attention, the only instrument
Able to dissipate the mind and its turmoil,
Shattering any expectations.

Attention has no center and no bounds, it is not
conditioned,
It is not "something" to be pursued, it cannot be
anticipated;
In fact, It is a quality of the "Divine Particle",
Appearing spontaneously, an action in Itself.

With the Light of clarity, It dissipates all that It
encounters,
The entire fragmentary mind;
Detached from time and space, it melts into Eternity,
Life itself provides it, through movement – simplicity.

We are one with Attention, listening and watching
All that Life brings us in the present moment;
Without It, we are at the mercy of thoughts,
disappointments and sorrow,
Unable to understand true Wisdom.

The Sacred or God is the Source of Life; It breathes energy
and life into the whole existence. It permeates all and
everything as Absolute Love. It has no beginning, It was
not created by anyone and It will never die. It was, is and
will always be immortal Existence, through Itself and by
Itself.

It contains both the quality of stillness, as well as that of eternal movement. It affirms Itself as Beauty, Kindness and limitless Love. It does not force, impose or compel anyone or anything, for Its patience is infinite. Both in the case of human beings, as well as with everything that exists, It does not impose Its authority or law, because in Its quality as Perfection It gives everyone freedom and, when needed, It helps the whole of creation satisfy its basic necessities.

The imaginary individual mind cannot encounter It, in any circumstance, because the "ego" cannot encompass that which is all-encompassing. Separating from It or trying to understand It with the knowing mind are acts of impiety.

Only the Sacred can affirm: "I Am". The rest are and will always remain mere fantasies of the mind. No durable or hallowing action can be performed in Its absence. The real meaning of Existence is demonstrated and sustained only by Its obvious Reality, on all levels of manifestation of the created world. No matter how much we try to explain, words are and will always be powerless, unable to grasp Uniqueness.

Let us return to the practice of what the author describes. How can we encounter It in a real way, without deceiving ourselves? Each person needs to constantly ask this question. In fact, It is within each of us, therefore very close; nevertheless It only affirms Itself in a completely silent mind. Silence alone can open Its path and, simultaneously, our whole being affirms itself as absolute newness. Here, we refer to a spontaneous and boundless silence – not wanted or forced in any way.

Can our individual mind – with its usual instruments – accomplish such silence? Of course not. The true silence we refer to is attained in simplicity, with the help of all-encompassing Attention, which has no center, no bounds and does not pursue a purpose or goal.

In fact, Attention is a quality of the Sacred existent within each human being; Its simple appearance is a transformative action. It is like a Sun, illuminating the whole field of consciousness, dissipating any darkness or shadows existent within the limited sphere of the "ego".

Therefore, united with Attention, we just listen to and watch everything that Life brings us in the present moment. In this state, the reactions of the mind are dissipated and they disappear; simultaneously, we have a pure thinking in which Love and Intelligence define us as timeless beings, functioning on the level of Divine Perfection.

Happiness Is Revealed in the Death of the Past

We encounter Happiness only when the past vanishes,
It manifests Itself spontaneously, intertwined with Love,
It is boundless, therefore It has no motivations,
We cannot search for It with the knowing mind.

Functioning as "ego", we encounter false happiness,
Created by the thinking process.
It is always connected to an achievement, a success,
An ephemeral satisfaction which can vanish the next
moment.

Finding a new goal to chase,
Constantly agitated, man weaves his sad fate;
Striving for happiness will always have relative results,
It chains us with its deceptive fulfillment.

When we watch the "ego" and its turmoil,
Constantly creating problems, pursuing happiness,
Exposed, it becomes completely silent – surprised by
                                    Enlightenment,
In the "psychological emptiness" our being is perpetually
                                    renewed.

In this circumstance – as absolute purity,
The whole being is transformed, it is newly born, in the
                                    moment,
United with the Sacredness of Life – boundless happiness,
Living and perceiving the mystery of the perfect moment.

Throughout his entire existence, man as an incarnated
being is in a permanent – conscious or unconscious –
search for happiness. But as long as we function as an
egocentric fragment, we will only be able to encounter a
flimsy, false happiness, always created by the thinking
process.

Conditioned by time and space – through education –
we associate happiness with facts, events or successes; they
are nothing but ephemeral satisfactions. Because we desire
happiness as a permanent state, its disappearance plunges
us into despair. Therefore, we resume our search for
happiness, by choosing another goal to pursue. In this
manner, we ourselves create a life filled with sorrow,

constantly oscillating, either towards fictitious hope, or towards desperation or frustration – vacillating in a state of duality.

As long as we live within the limited dimension of the "personal self", any search for happiness is relative and destined to fail, for it is based, from the very beginning, on deceitful achievements.

If we simply watch the struggle and turmoil of the "ego" – constantly agitated, creating many problems in its pursuit of true happiness – as we expose it with the rays of Attention, it is instantly dissipated.

From now on, our being – in a state of no-mind – becomes whole and, as "Pure Consciousness", we are united with the Sacredness of the Aliveness in Its eternal movement. In this state, we encounter true Happiness, moment to moment, which has no connection to the ephemeral aspects of the limited world.

To conclude, we can only encounter immortal Happiness in the total absence of the past as "self" or "personal ego". The mind, no matter how cultured, can never encounter Happiness, because its very presence obstructs the apparition of this wonderful phenomenon.

The Pause

Between thoughts and words, no matter how fast they
are uttered,
There is always an interval – a pause without thoughts,
Laden with mystery. In this silence,
There is true comprehension, beyond the "ego"
Created by time, through formulas and imagination.

Our life and the Universe obey this law
Of movement and rest; therefore, we need
To understand it through a direct experience,
By melting into the moment.

This blissful encounter turns children into giants,
The fire of suffering perishes, all conflicts disappear,
Created by thinking and fueled by time.
Silence is, in fact, the "Nothingness", elevating us
ceaselessly
On the ascending spiral, into the Immense Boundlessness.

When we understand this mechanism from personal
experience:
All the time, in any place, in any circumstance,
With a lucid Attention we try to encompass the moment
Of stillness, rest, no-thought between thoughts and words.

This is – simply – the whole mystery of "Self-knowing",
The only way to save the human being
From his aberrant recordings, turning life into an inferno.

The pause between thoughts and words is of utmost importance in "Self-knowing". No matter how quickly the process of thinking or speaking takes place, we discover that there is an interval between words or thoughts, a pause of no-thought or psychological passiveness, laden with mystery. In fact, the very light of this "psychological void" enables us to understand the meaning of the words as cerebral memories. Therefore, thanks to these pauses, we grasp the meaning as an effect of the known.

In our life, as well as everywhere in the Universe, the Universal Law of Movement and Rest operates. We can only understand it from personal experience, through a direct contact with the freshness of each moment. In this happy encounter with the eternal newness of the moment, ignorant children become true giants, understanding the Sublime Truth. This correct encounter dissipates any suffering, contradiction or conflict generated and sustained by dysfunctional thinking.

The silence or "psychological Nothingness" is our constant companion on the path of moral and spiritual evolution, until we return to our home, the Source of the Sacred, from where we descended once in order to experience the world of matter. As soon as we find out about this mystery and its beneficial effects, we also need to put this knowledge into practice.

Therefore, in any circumstance we find ourselves, with a lucid Attention, let us try – persistently – to encounter Life in present moments. Functioning as "One", as Pure Consciousness, let us always be "here and now". Only on this level of authentic peace can the human being be saved from his flimsy conditioning, which turns life into a living inferno.

Searching for the Unknown

We can only search for what we already know or imagine
In the mirror of the mind – a mere fiction.
The "Unknown" and the "search" exclude one another,
They are mere symbols, which need to be dropped.

Newness – un-encountered before – is an eternal mystery,
It requests of us to be just as new.
Fresh, new, unused brain cells
Can comprehend it and understand it as perfection.

Therefore, the arrogant mind and its knowledge needs to
be silent,
For it creates falsehood, through the imaginary "ego";
All-encompassing Attention dissipates the ideal fiction
And it disappears...

In the peace that ensues,
Without purpose, will or desire,
The Infinite absorbs us
And we experience the Unknown.

As the moment dies,
A spontaneous encounter –
In a flash, it melts,
We are eternally free.

Any search is connected to the known:
Images, imagination, fantasies of the past.
Do not be deceived,
If you want to be liberated!

With our knowing mind we can only search for that which we already know. Finding is nothing but a recognition of something we have known previously, preserved as an image on the film of memory, stored at the level of the astral body.

Let us see how memory is recorded. Through the five senses, we receive all kinds of information from the surrounding environment. Through the sense organs and the nervous system, this information reaches the neural-cerebral system and the astral brain. According to the information we receive, we will take certain decisions. In this process of perception and decision, we use a large quantity of brain cells, which can be used only once; therefore, no other information can be recorded in them. These brain cells store and record the images of past experiences, enabling us to recognize them.

From this perspective, the Unknown and the search are symbols which exclude each other and can never be associated. Let us abandon these symbols and see how we can encounter the Unknown, for It is an eternal mystery, determined by the perpetual movement and freshness of the Aliveness.

In order to be able to encounter this newness, we have to welcome it according to its qualities. Therefore, we need to use new brain cells, unused before, able to understand newness in a real way. Our old, knowing mind needs to become silent, as well as all its recorded memory, for the encounter of the old with the new can only distort understanding.

Therefore, the old mind, based on used brain cells, must be silent. Does it become silent at our command? Of course not! But if we point the watchful, all-encompassing Light-Attention towards it, we discover that the simplicity of this encounter dissipates any thinking process. Its disappearance is natural, for all its material is made up of hollow images, empty of content. As Attention illuminates them, they are dispelled in a flash.

In that moment of peace or "psychological emptiness", a new mind, of universal proportions, with new cerebral cells comes into action and encounters and comprehends the Unknown.

Let us explain this phenomenon from the perspective of "Self-knowing". When the reactions of the mind are encountered with the rays of Attention, they disappear and the peace of the soul ensues. In that moment, new cerebral cells start to function and to record the new. Simultaneously, we are absorbed into Infinity; melting into It, we experience the Unknown, which immediately becomes old. Repeating this encounter as freshness will offer us another moment of liberation, enabling us to encounter the

Unknown, in syntony with the movement of the Aliveness.

Let us remember that any search is connected to the known, to our past, as an image or a fantasy. We can only dissolve this past – which brought us into reincarnation – by simply becoming aware of it; Attention – the Sacred itself in action – dissipates it.

Mystical Ecstasy

Through images and formulas, repeated ceaselessly,
Will pursues a goal, as a struggling "ego",
Many misinterpreted phenomena occur,
Deemed as a manifestation of the divine – the human
being as sacred.

In such circumstance, the "self" is always present,
Trapped in time and space – the individual, perfectly
conscious,
Is separated from what he perceives: as subject
and object,
Duality is still present, with its old intellect.

A form of so-called ecstasy – man is separate from
the divine,
He experiences enthusiasm, emotions and satisfaction;
Drunk with success, he increases his self-importance,
Projected on peaks, he admires his false godliness.

The visions are an effect of his beliefs,
According to his faith, based on the memory baggage;
All of these happen within the confines of the "ego",
created by time,
A deceitful phenomenon; psychologically, the illusion
grows.

The real mystical ecstasy has different characteristics:
Completely detached from the fantasies of the "ego",
There is no duality, the "ego" is totally absent,
Man – outside time and space – is completely
independent.

There is no purpose, no expectations, no assessments,
There is no previous preparation through acts of will;
It appears spontaneously, in its perfection,
Silence and harmony – a sacred climate of fulfillment.

Encountering "Pure Consciousness", manifested as Light,
The instrument – all-encompassing Attention;
Practically, It is ecstasy – uninfluenced
By the possessive mind and the conditioned individual.

In such a state, we fully experience, directly,
Complete Oneness,
Melting into the Great Energy, where everything
originated,
Love and Happiness ensue, simultaneously with the
death of the "ego".

A well-trained will, obsessively repeating images and formulas, can give the "ego" the ability to materialize certain phenomena. To name but a few: clairvoyance, clairaudience, astral journeying, levitation, stigmata etc. All of these are wrongly considered to be manifestations of the Divine in that particular individual. Generally, they create self-importance, vanity, pride and arrogance. Based on these abilities, some individuals are declared to be saints after their death and honored as such.

In all these external manifestations, the "self" is always present, limited by time and space, and he is aware of that particular ability as something separate. Therefore, there is a subject and an object, a duality created by the intellect.

Among these phenomena, we also encounter the so-called mystical ecstasy. In this circumstance, the experiencer is still in a state of duality. He experiences moments of enthusiasm, emotions and complete satisfaction, which give him an illusion of success and the arrogance that he is a godly being.

These visions are closely connected to the practitioner's faith. A Christian will have a vision of Jesus or Mother Mary, a Buddhist will encounter the Enlightened Buddha etc. All of these are mere deceitful apparitions, for they take place within the shell of mental baggage which creates the structure of the "ego".

There is – undoubtedly – a real state of ecstasy. Here are

the signs which confirm its reality: the "ego" or "personal self" has completely disappeared, with all its baggage; therefore, there is no duality. The blissful experiencer lives outside time and space, completely independent, integrated into the Great Energy. This ecstasy cannot be prepared or anticipated in any way. There is no purpose or ideal to accomplish; also, there is no subject who can assess and interpret the phenomenon.

Ecstasy appears in a climate of Silence and inner harmony. It appears spontaneously, and lucid, impersonal Attention dissipates all the obstacles in its path.

In this state we function as a whole being, integrated into the Great and Unique Love. We are "Pure Consciousness", Love and boundless Happiness. All of these occur simultaneously with the death or unconditional shattering of the "ego".

Do Not Try to Be Simple

Psychologically, simplicity is incomparable, indescribable,
A priceless value, it ensues indirectly, as an effect.
Any attempt to be simple, through effort and
                                imagination,
Can only create despair, a cartoon of the real man.

The mind which attempts to achieve simplicity through
                                                    struggle
Is a mind created by time – one with duality;
On the one hand, the "ego" on the other, the imaginary
                                                        fact;
Between them, the struggle, striving towards the goal.

The approach is wrong from the very beginning,
For we act through the "ego", a limited structure,
Unable to encounter that which is true and real,
For it is always old – a creation of time.

If you see and understand this, through living experience,
Not just intellectually, but as a direct encounter,
Any such attempts are pointless, destined to fail,
Spontaneously, you experience real integration.

The whole being – as one – melting into Infinity,
You move and act in a perfect way,
One with the eternal movement of the Reality of Life,
In a perfect order, a blissful communion.

Here is how – without any acts of will – you attain
                                                simplicity,
Through it, spontaneously, you also attain Reality;
From now on, on this level of "being", always present
You move and act as an independent "Whole".

Only thus do you encounter Happiness without cause,
It is stillness, unblemished and untouched by anything;
If we live in the "now", in union with the moment,
Holy Action manifests itself.

Our transformation ensues without any desire or will,
Through the so-called passiveness, the "ego" perishes;
Each moment encountered directly dissipates its structure,
In time, its whole fiction disintegrates completely.

Holy simplicity, innocence and humbleness, unforced in any way, are undeniable qualities experienced as a summum by whoever practices "Self-knowing".

A self-important mind trying to attain simplicity through efforts of will is nothing but a desperate, confused and ignorant mind. It functions in a fragmentary, dualistic way. On the one side, the fictitious "ego" on the other, the imaginary simplicity. The individual tries to reduce the gulf between reality and the imaginary ideal through efforts of will and permanent desires. But these are nothing but conflictual states, noise and suffering.

By simply exposing this erroneous practice, we instantly detach from it. The moment the egoistic entity ceases its activity, the mind – in complete humbleness – is absorbed into the infinity of the "psychological emptiness". From now on, the being, completely free from the obsessive past, experiences wholeness and integrity and, united with the Reality of Life, he acts in a perfect way, in perfect harmony.

In this manner – without any efforts on our part – we experience simplicity and inner aloneness, and we act as an independent "Whole", in a permanent present, moment after moment in their eternal newness and freshness. Only in this circumstance do we encounter Happiness without cause, which is and will remain our permanent reality when we function as a complete being, "here and now", in constant union with the moment.

The transformation of our egoistic being – a creation of time – can only be accomplished in this state of humble passiveness. The state of no-mind gradually weakens the authority of the "ego"; finally, its whole structure collapses. The surprise phenomenon of Liberation from the cage of egoism is marked by a new life, in which creative Love leads our whole being through intuitive impulses.

Let us remember, therefore, that we cannot attain simplicity through the means of the "ego", but only by exposing it as the cause of the entire human tragedy and misery. Both the exposure and the dissolution of the "ego" are accomplished with the help of lucid, impersonal, all-encompassing Attention. This all-inclusive Attention is the Sacred within us, existent through Itself, by Itself.

The Conflict between the Observer and the Observed

Encountering "what is" is not easy,
Yet the phenomenon is accessible to all individuals
Who want to understand themselves
Through experience and real action.

Let us see what happens, in an all-encompassing contact
With people, things, facts or nature in general;
How we watch and listen to the permanent challenge,
In connection with movement, evident through itself.

Between the eye which observes and the observed object,
The observer sneaks in, with its assessments and opinions,
Based on the memory structure,
Bringing the whole past into the present.

Thus, there is a conflict between the real present
And the unreal image of yesterday,
Which criticizes, compares, disapproves or accepts,
A true encounter becomes impossible.

Therefore, the observer is the imaginary "ego",
Preventing the contact with life's mysterious gifts,
Creating contradiction, conflicts and pain;
All the suffering of the world originates from its presence.

Through all-encompassing Attention, you see it, totally,
The very moment it appears – as a lucid knower;
By exposing it spontaneously, without any goals
                              or expectations,
This non-action makes it disappear.

When the observer vanishes, observation appears;
It is a simple watching, clear and penetrating,
Which encompasses and comprehends, renewing itself
each moment,
It is both life and death, in an eternal movement.

A direct relationship – a state of communion,
The integral being is without dimensions,
A timeless structure, boundless harmony,
Without cause-effect, free from images.

In this realm of freedom, we become Love,
Not the love we search for in some form, as a fulfillment;
We are one with Love – a hallowing state,
By itself, through itself, it transforms our deceitful nature.

The encounter with the reality of Life – absolute freshness
and newness from one moment to another – is not easy. But
for a serious practitioner who understands the value of this
experience, everything will unfold naturally. The simplicity
of the encounter with "what is" happens effortlessly, and it
becomes, through itself, an obvious transformative action,
a support and an invitation to experience "Self-knowing".

Let us see what really happens in our encounter with
our fellow beings, with things, facts and with nature in
general.

How do we watch and listen to the permanent challenge
brought forth by the movement of life in its diversity and
wholeness?

Here is what we discover. Between the sense organ
which watches and listens, and the object we watch or

listen to – an observer or listener appears, arising from the memory content. This apparition distorts the correct understanding of the present phenomenon; there is a conflict between the obsolete and outdated old and the real, alive and present new. In other words, the memory reactions – recordings of previous experiences – distort the understanding of the present in its natural unfoldment in moments of existence. Because of this interference, there is an obvious conflict between the real and active present and the image of past experiences. As this fiction appears, the contact with the present moment is interrupted and our attention is drawn to the assessments of the past – the observer who criticizes, accepts or disapproves.

Therefore, understanding is impossible as long as we encounter the present through the memories of the past.

This intruder, the observer, is, in fact, the "ego", whose structure is made up of outdated, old elements, images of previous experiences. The "ego" is guilty of all the confusion the soul is experiencing.

All conflictual states originate from this structure made of memories – in the present moment mere dead images, lifeless fictions – as well as all the suffering and sorrow which degrade us morally and deteriorate the health of our physical body.

The cult of the "ego", sustained by the savage greed of personal goals, is the cause of all the suffering and chaos existent today on planet Earth, as a true epidemic affecting all social layers.

If you have reached the same conclusions, from your own experience, it means that, by yourself, you have found the path towards truth.

By becoming conscious of this intruder, it is eventually dissipated. Any fiction illuminated by the spontaneous sparkle of Attention is instantly dissolved, without leaving any memory residues.

Practically, a direct encounter with the observer makes it disappear; all that is left is pure observation, which, through itself and by itself, is both understanding and action.

The lived moment is forgotten, in order to be able to welcome and encounter the next moment with the same simplicity. It is a true experience and a psychological death, in eternal movement.

Thus, as complete beings, in perfect harmony, in a timeless state, we encounter and understand the reality and beauty of life. Only on this level of experience – as a wonderful simplicity – do we encounter Love, overflowing its beneficial purity onto us, transforming egoism and the whole hideousness of worldly vanities.

The Earthquake

In the course of my existence, I experienced three major earthquakes. In this instance as well – just like in any other parts of this book – I am describing a phenomenon I experienced and encountered directly.

The mysterious, muffled sound, rising from the depths of the earth, the buildings shaking uncontrollably, moving the furniture and other objects in an eerie, diabolical dance, create a climate of terror for humans as well as for other living creatures.

As the focus of our interest is the human being, let us try to describe both his chaotic attitude when faced with an earthquake, as well as the correct approach we need to take in order to avoid and deal with its inherent dangers.

An ordinary man, used to encountering the movement of life with his arrogant mind – the self-important knowing entity – will automatically approach the earthquake with the same mind. After the initial surprise caused by the phenomenon, he will feel distressed; immediately afterwards, distress turns into panic. The reactions of the mind will direct his actions in a self-centered way. He will try either to save things or people he is attached to, or his own person. Each initiative will be erroneously directed by the "ego".

Here are a few examples, events that actually took place. Someone jumped out of the window, forgetting that he lived on a high floor. Another person dashed to the staircase, which fell on top of him. While leaving his house in a hurry, a man was killed by a brick falling from the chimney onto his head.

In all these cases, they would have survived the earthquake, had they not left the room.

The thinking process, based on ordinary knowledge from old and outdated past experiences, recorded in the memory, will provide corresponding solutions. Thus, the person is detached from the present and he projects himself into the past, repeating an old experience in his imagination.

By using the thinking mind, it is impossible to understand the present moment, life's activity in permanent movement, as absolute newness.

The earthquake, as a phenomenon of high intensity and surprise, represents a wonderful opportunity to become integrated into the present.

Being "one" with the movement of the earthquake means, first of all, becoming detached from the conformist mind, a creation of the past, and being integrated into the reality of the present.

In this state of stillness, the Sacred within us – through wise intuitive impulses – will suggest what we need to do in order to save our lives, the lives of others, as well as the rest of our goods.

Intelligence Is Oneness

Intellect and Intelligence are two completely different
                                                    states,
Both present in man on different levels of understanding.
Intellect is the "ego" or the mentality,
It is different from individual to individual, fueled by
                                            self-importance.

Created throughout time, conditioned psychologically,
The intellect is in conflict with itself and others,
                                    ceaselessly egocentric;
Seeking pleasure and avoiding pain,
Its constant motivation.

Here, there is no light, just permanent darkness,
All man does through the "ego" results in misery.
When the intellect is silent – the thinking mind stops,
Seeing its powerlessness, it becomes humble.

Thus we discover Sacred Innocence, free from limitations,
On this level, man is a creative being.
Psychologically, we are all the same, Intelligence is One,
Through it, we are Oneness, of divine origin.

United with Eternity, we express ourselves through Love,
Living each moment in a perfect way.
Only here do we encounter true Happiness,
Only in this climate – the being is holy.

In current speech, a confusion is often made between these
two notions: Intelligence and intellect.

In fact, these two concepts express completely different
meanings. Furthermore, they exist on different levels of
manifestation.

The intellect is part of the realm of the "ego" or the
surface consciousness. Therefore, it is created and
sustained by accumulations of memory. It is a creation of
time, manifesting itself egocentrically, and it is always in
conflict with itself, as well as with the external world. It
makes all its decisions based on motivations related to
pleasure or pain.

Functioning on this level, the human being will never
know true peace or the true meaning of life. The more the
intellect knows, the more the "ego" becomes arrogant and
the moral degradation of the individual deepens.

If we expose the intellect and its origin, as well as its
dysfunctional patterns – in the light of Attention – it
becomes completely silent. In its absence, we encounter the
silence or peace of the soul, which is boundless, beyond
any models or patterns.

From now on, in a state of stillness, we encounter
Intelligence – a quality of the Divine within us – leading us
through intuitive impulses. This Intelligence is Oneness
and it manifests itself as "Perfection". It is common to all
human beings. At the level of Intelligence, all individuals
have the same understanding and use the same creative
thinking; they express themselves through Love and

experience Happiness beyond dimensions.

It is only in this climate of harmony, by experiencing Intelligence and its hallowing effects, that we also influence the rest of the world accordingly.

Listening and Watching

Listening and watching directly, in simplicity,
Correctly applied, it leads to fulfillment.
Neither past nor future participate in this encounter,
The mind, absolutely humble, melts into Immortality.

In silence, the whole being is absorbed into Infinity
Beyond time and space, the "ego" is shattered,
We encounter the Unnamable – One Reality,
Cleansing and transforming our natural being.

In this experience, the ancestral residues are dissolved,
They have brought us on Earth to expiate our karma.
The simplicity and frequency of these encounters
Will create visible effects, leading to fulfillment.

One day, the "self" will lose its precarious energies,
All this happens in simplicity, a natural integration,
When we are Love – perfection dwelling in each of us,
An all-encompassing perception, accessible to everyone.

We use Attention in every circumstance,
Its effects heal and ennoble us;
It is the Sacred in action, through impulses of Love,
Ceaselessly, it reveals the state of Happiness.

The correct practice of "Self-knowing" requires, from the very beginning, that we learn the art of listening and watching. Both are performed in absolute simplicity. The mind and its memory accumulations are completely excluded. The whole secret consists of listening and watching, with the flame of lucid Attention, dissipating any reactions of the mind.

As the mind becomes silent, in humbleness, spontaneously, our being becomes One. In that moment, our being, the state of Pure Consciousness and all-encompassing Love melt into one harmonious Whole, uniting us with Eternity.

In order to facilitate understanding and simplify practice, we will provide further explanations. Listening and watching directly, without any interference from the memorial past, we need only one instrument: a lucid, watchful, spontaneous and disinterested Attention. In fact, Attention is the Sacred within us; It illuminates and dissipates the memory residues, creating hallowing transformations. Therefore, with the help of Attention, we will encounter the chaotic activity of the mind, vacillating continuously between past and future, under the effect of automatic memory impulses.

The simplicity of this encounter spontaneously dissipates the pointless wandering of the mind. In the "psychological void" which ensues naturally, the Sacred existent in the depth of our being is united with the One Reality. From now on, in this state, without intervening in any way, the depth of our being is purified. Only in this circumstance are all the ancestral residues eliminated, as they brought us to our present incarnation in order to expiate immoral deeds we have done in our past lives.

Any individual who is serious and honest with himself can discover – on his own, through practice – this visible and clear experience, the effects of this simplicity as a true reality, unfolding on the always ascending path of spiritual evolution. The frequency of these unprogrammed and undesired encounters dissolves and eliminates the energies of the "personal self", whose prisoner we are for the time being – without pursuing this in any shape or form.

One day, no one can foretell when, we will encounter and experience the phenomenon of Enlightenment or Liberation. This fortunate phenomenon does not happen gradually – today a little bit, tomorrow a bit more – but spontaneously. In my own experience, this phenomenon occurred during sleep. When he awakens, the fortunate mortal discovers – to his absolute surprise – that he functions completely differently than before.

After this true surgery, performed on the ordinary human psyche, all the fragmentary energies which held us prisoners in the cage of the "ego" are naturally and spontaneously eliminated. Each problem caused by the perpetual movement of Life is solved instantly, as intuition provides us with the best solutions, in a flash. We encounter everything that the movement of the Aliveness brings indiscriminately, whether pleasant or painful. Each event is a wonderful opportunity to transcend from the limited dimension of the "ego", melting with Divinity.

In this state, Love intertwined with Happiness define our existence in a way that is difficult or even impossible to describe in words. But we try, nevertheless, so that the reader can have an approximate understanding of the phenomenon. We call that moment "direct Knowing" – a direct experience of the Absolute Truth.

Life and Death – Just a Detachment

Why do you cry and mourn, psychologically
                                    traumatized?
Has someone dear to you died: a relative, a friend,
                                    a lover?
Do you cry for the person who detached from Earth,
                                    fulfilling a law,
Or maybe you cry for yourself, as you miss the departed?

These questions are an invitation to self-inquiry!
When man does not truly know himself,
He is just a machine, led by his conditioning,
Deeply rooted inherited limited patterns of thinking
Centered in the "self"!

When he is not a whole man – all he sees or thinks,
His actions are chaotic and confused.
There is, in fact, no death, just a detachment,
We leave the body as one discards a coat,
When it is damaged through degradation or a certain
accident.

The Aliveness – essential being – never disappears,
Detached from Its physical support, It is practically
liberated
From the dark pit holding It prisoner
And is reborn into a different world, with wider horizons.
For man, this discovery is of utmost importance!

If man knew this truth, there would be no fear of death,
He would approach life differently, with more simplicity.
Let us see how we can prove this statement,
Each of you, try this experiment for yourselves!

We start the inquiry with another question:
What is man, in a true sense, besides the physical body?
A collection of knowledge, information and faiths,
Personal experiences, various attachments
To people and possessions, to a social position,
A certain title or a name;
This is the ordinary condition of man on planet Earth.

How does he function? Egocentrically, in constant turmoil,
Never content, rarely happy,
Unable to understand the true meaning of Life.

If we simply encounter – each for himself –
This way of "being", in relationship with Life,
Without any expectations or imaginary goals,
This simple meeting liberates us spontaneously
From the past, from the psychological content,
Conditioned by time.

What remains, in the "void" that ensues?
Only "psychological emptiness" – through it – we are
                                        Superconscious,
Without center, without bounds, alive, lucid, active and
                                        present.
This alive, active Reality in movement,
Ensuing spontaneously as the old disappears,
Proves – beyond doubt – that the "Aliveness" within us
                                        never dies!

We cannot comprehend and understand Life,
Unless the past – the memory content – disappears.
Life and death are one movement – the meaning of
                                        existence,
They are always united, there is no separation.

By experiencing and understanding this self-inquiry,
Fear of death disappears in that very moment.
When we leave the body – our carnal structure,
The state of presence in the moment is necessary in the
                                        "beyond" as well,
In order to perfectly encounter that reality.
Evolution demands that we leave the old, the outdated,
And encounter Eternity and Its transforming power.

Why do you cry and sigh, why all these traumatic negative psychosomatic effects because a loved one has died? Do you cry for the one who detached from planet Earth – following his destiny – or do you cry for yourself, as you miss the departed? Ask yourself these questions, inquire within! When man does not understand his manner of functioning, he responds to the movement of Life automatically, from his memory baggage. As a being trapped in time-space and limited by the "ego", he sees, judges and acts confusingly and chaotically, according to the patterns of psychological conditioning.

In fact, there is no death in the true sense of the word. The so-called death is a mere separation of the Aliveness from the body, from the planetary piece of clothing; as it has become damaged, we are unable to continue our existence as incarnated beings.

The Aliveness – pure and eternal essence – never disappears. As it becomes detached from the physical body, it is reborn in a different dimension called the astral world. Discovering this truth is of utmost importance, in order to understand the true meaning of existence as a human being in a carnal body. In this context, fear of death loses its importance, and we approach Life with much more simplicity.

Let us see if this statement can be discovered by each individual, through a direct experience. Let us inquire: what is the human being beyond the body? A bundle of knowledge, information, faiths, attachments, social position, fame etc. This is the reality of the ordinary man, functioning egocentrically, in constant turmoil. Generally, he is never content. He rarely experiences serenity, the only state able to provide the chance to understand the true meaning of life.

How can we eliminate the obstacles which prevent true

understanding? Practically, only by coming into contact – each for himself – with our behavior in relationship with Life, without pursuing any purpose, ideal, advantage or expectation. Through this simple encounter, our psychological structure becomes silent; in this silence, we discover that we nevertheless exist as a state of all-encompassing, alive, lucid, active and perpetually present Superconsciousness.

This Reality, as a state of serenity – attentive and lucid Pure Consciousness – appears spontaneously, as the old disappears – and it proves, beyond any doubt, that the Aliveness within us never dies! We cannot understand and encompass Life in Its Reality unless the whole past – the memory baggage – disappears.

Therefore, psychologically, Life-death – united as "One", as one single movement – enables us to discover the mysteries of Existence. If you have correctly understood this text, fear of death will completely disappear throughout your existence as an incarnated being, as well as in that fatal moment when you shall leave your clothing made of clay. The state of passiveness of the mind or lucid presence – accomplished through a direct contact with the present moment with the help of lucid, all-encompassing Attention – can also be experienced in the "beyond", in the astral world.

Our moral and spiritual evolution requires that we leave that which is old and outdated, in order to encounter Eternity with Its beneficial, transformative effects.

Listening to Silence

Silence, peace, rest, inner order,
A priceless harmony, unfolding within us,
Express themselves through a sound with hallowing
                                                    effects,
It is the song of the Soul – a sublime transformation.

All the mysteries of Life are hidden within silence,
Under this continuous sound, melting with the Aliveness;
Some rarely hear it, some listen to it frequently,
The external noise is temporarily diluted.

Living in this state, we are in meditation,
A state of Pure Awakening, as a blessing;
Love, Beauty, Kindness and Joy
Are the effects of its very essence.

In this circumstance, we and the Divine are One,
For we have the same Source – a Sublime Perfection,
Our purpose in this world is to unite as one,
Creating a new world, in perfect harmony.

In "Self-knowing", silence is our guide to fulfillment,
When the illusion disappears, without any struggle,
Illuminated by all-encompassing Attention,
All is dissipated; in its place, all-inclusive peace ensues.

In this "psychological void", we are extended into Infinity,
We live hallowing moments, melting into the Sublime.
This is how we can accomplish the true purpose of our
                                        incarnation,
In Union with the Whole – when the "ego" melts away.

Inner silence as harmony, peace, rest and total independence is a true divine blessing; in this state, we directly
experience Happiness, free from any external motivations.
The mind is silent, in humbleness, as it has understood its
intrinsic powerlessness. The body is filled with energy,
allowing it to regenerate its damaged cells, which had
deteriorated in one's efforts to provide what is necessary
for survival.

As body, mind and spirit become "One", the individual
who truly experiences this communion perceives an inner
subtle sound. This sound accompanies the mysterious
process of the Aliveness on its return journey to the Sacred
Source, from which, eons ago, it descended in order to
experience the world of matter in its various forms of
manifestation.

Living on this plane, we are a State of Awakening, accessible to all Souls, as human beings. It is only in this state
that we encounter Kindness, Beauty, Truth, Joy and
boundless Happiness. If even one of these qualities is
present, It will also attract all the others; the individual
does not need to resort to his memory baggage, as a self-

important "ego".

By totally melting with Divinity, in moments of existence, the individual makes a leap towards perfection; through him, the whole Universe also makes this leap. The world can only be perfected by starting from the perfection of each of its components, that is, of each individual.

This wonderful phenomenon can be accomplished by each individual, regardless of his stage of evolution, for within all of us there is the same Spark, which detached from Divinity and was sent into the material world in order to make the experience of that which is fleeting and perishable.

Practically, we realize this state by using the Light-Attention; we simply encounter our erroneous way of functioning, based on illusions, which dominates all beings who live an egocentric, fragmentary life, tied to that which is fleeting, imaginary and without any real support.

Timelessness

The past and the future are completely absent,
In this authentic experience.
A state of "being" present "here and now"
Or Pure Consciousness – living independently.

Untroubled by the mind, the complete blissful man,
Body and mind as one – a silent, perfect Wholeness,
One with Life, in perpetual movement,
From one moment to another, a creative freshness.

Beyond time and space lies Reality,
Beyond body and mind – united with the Immensity;
We are just an authentic needle-point, a dot of Light,
In constant connection with the Divine Greatness.

This is, in fact, the state of Timelessness,
The worldly and the "ego" perish;
Its existence is confirmed only through authentic
                                                experience,
If we try to describe it in words, it immediately
                                                disappears.

The thought, the word as language brings us
Back to the dimension of time, chained by the mind;
Being and not being are ephemeral states,
Alternating glimpses of fullness.

Physically and mentally, there is a beginning and an end,
In Reality – all is eternal and endless;
We melt into the infinite present,
We encounter and become one with Love.

This is who we really are – our essence is Love,
The essence of our real nature is perfection, through itself
and by itself,
It affirms itself spontaneously when the personality
disappears,
With all its illusions and lies.

"Self-knowing" gives us the possibility to be timeless,
In communion with the Aliveness, in the present,
in the now;
Attention is the efficient instrument
Which demolishes the past – the eternal obstacle.

The simplicity of this encounter with our "ego"
Requires no effort or struggle – just a natural encounter;
It is beyond imagination, beyond expectation,
Simply watching the mind – a direct contact.

Learn to Completely Die to Yourself

If you want to be a whole human being, absolutely
independent,
Able to perceive what is now, real and present,
You must completely die to yourself,
The mind – created by time – needs to be silent through
non-action!

The moment of non-action comes through perception,
A direct encounter with everything that appears in the
moment;
We just watch and listen to everything we encounter –
attentively –
Free from past and future, we are integrated in the "now".

Life is perpetual freshness, in permanent movement,
As such, we need to be the same way;
A childlike innocence is requested by Existence,
Every time, in every circumstance – a priceless purity.

The psychological death provides the wonderful perspective
Of encountering Reality each moment, as uniqueness;
The vessel of consciousness is empty of all content,
This is the supreme condition for this encounter.

Are you afraid to die to all you have accumulated?
Who is the fearful entity? Is it real or imaginary?
Our duty is to inquire, each for himself,
Personal experience is of utmost importance.

Fear and the word "death" go together,
Fear is a real phenomenon, its shiver shakes our being;
The moment it arises, it is just a feeling,
But in the following moment, the fearful entity also
appears.

It is, in fact, a fiction, created by thought,
Dividing our being into imagination and reality;
The fearful entity is always the "ego" – as past and
                                                    future,
Creating states of tension, as it loves conflict.

If we encounter fear in the incoming moment,
Using Attention, as an accompanying Light,
It immediately disappears and we disappear as well,
We die to all that was, as well as to all that we possess.

Through this death, we encounter liberation,
United with the Infinite, we are creative beings;
We die each moment and we are reborn in perfect
                                                    harmony,
Creating a new world, based on Love.

Life is a perfectly functional "Whole", in perpetual
mobility and freshness from one moment to another. In
order to understand It, we need to welcome It the same
way It is: as whole human beings, with a new, humble
mind, uncontaminated by any previous recordings.

Therefore we need to encounter Life as complete beings,
with a perpetually innocent mind.

Do we encounter Life in this manner? Not at all.
Conditioned by the education we have received, we
function as an egoistic entity, as a fictitious "personal self",
based on what it knows or possesses. In other words, we
are an imaginary entity.

In order to discover and realize the real man, there is no
other way but to demolish this fictitious "ego". Here is

how: with the help of lucid Attention, we encounter the reactions of the mind, which created the "ego". This simple, direct and disinterested encounter makes it disappear; in the "void" that ensues, an immense empty space is created. In this psychological death, the vessel of consciousness is suddenly emptied; our mind is innocent and our being is full: body, mind and spirit functioning as a "Whole". In this happy state we are able to encounter Life's movement.

Are you afraid to die to all these cerebral memory recordings? But who is the entity who is afraid? Is it a reality, through itself and by itself, or is it just a frail fantasy?

We need to make this discovery ourselves. Let us never be content with what others have described, for only what we discover from personal experience has an extreme and unique significance.

Fear as an emotion and the word "death" go together. Fear is a real phenomenon; it creates anguish and stress within our being. The moment the fearful entity appears – as a fiction created by thought – our being is divided between the real and the imaginary.

The fearful entity is always the "ego" – as an image of the past or as a projection into the future. It is to blame for all tensional states; the moment the "ego" appears, a tensional state is created.

If we simply encounter fear with the light of lucid Attention, it disappears; with it, we also disappear as "ego"! Thus we die psychologically to everything that was and to everything that we wish to be.

This demise of the "ego" offers us moments of liberation; in this state – united with the Infinite – we are creative beings. We die and are reborn each living moment, in a perfect harmony, in constant contact with Eternity.

As our being is hallowed – without any acts of will on our part – a new world is created, guided by Love and creative Wisdom.

Pollution

The human physical body, created throughout eons,
Has a certain structure and natural behavior;
If there is peace within us – absolute harmony,
Body and mind are as one, living authentically.

Man is a real universe – millions of cells
In perpetual movement, maintaining life through
                                        strict laws,
The transformative impulse of the primordial cell
Towards a total integration with Divinity, as one breath.

Degradation is a consequence of lack of understanding,
A behavior based on ignorance and superstition;
Unhealthy food destroys our body,
Leading to an untimely death.

We also degrade the environment,
The air we breathe, increasingly poisonous,
Exhaust fumes, the ever-growing number of cars,
Traumatize our body with harmful effects.

The chemicals in the soil are also found in cereals,
Various insecticides are absorbed by plants,
Poison is stored in fruits and the people who eat them,
In this context, what we consume can be harmful.

Through chemical discharges, vegetation disappears,
Rivers, seas, as well as oceans are polluted;
Atomic experiments create further degradation,
A clear insanity, self-evident from its effects.

This destructive game played by man,
As powerful "ego", unaware of what is right or wrong,
Greed, pleasure, goals, arrogance and pride
Create excesses, resulting in death and calamities.

Seeing the countless errors and the ill-fated action,
We become attentive and lucid – led by Wisdom.
The Sacred is within all of us – a valuable advisor,
Humbleness is the path, so It can become our Teacher.

The human body has been meticulously created
throughout a lengthy process of evolution and it represents
a universe in itself. It has the inner capacity to respond
intelligently to any types of stimuli, either coming from the

external world or arising from the inner world. Nevertheless, the regenerative quality that the body is endowed with needs to be discovered and constantly practiced.

When this ability is missing, man behaves in a dysfunctional way; usual activities – which become habits through obsessive repetition – cause degradation both for himself and for the environment.

Besides eating unhealthy food, he is forced to live his daily life in a noxious environment. The air, absolutely vital for any living being, is constantly poisoned by exhaust fumes, as the number of cars continues to increase. A poisoned air will definitely have destructive effects on the respiratory system and the whole organism.

The human being also poisons himself with the chemicals and insecticides in the soil, which finally end up in the cereals and fruits that he consumes.

Rivers, lakes and oceans are polluted with chemical refuse. The flora and fauna of this planet are increasingly destroyed. Fish, shellfish and other sea animals are also poisoned; by eating them, man poisons his own body.

Nuclear experiments represent the peak of madness and arrogance; they only complete all the other degradations of nature, and man needs to face the consequences.

Who is guilty of the general pollution and degradation of the environment?

None other than the scientist, for he functions egocentrically, just like any ordinary human being. Hasty discoveries, insufficiently researched regarding their possible effects over a period of time, have led to the present tragic consequences and the general destruction of nature.

What can we do about all this?

First of all, each individual is endowed with inner mechanisms of adaptation. Some organisms are more adaptable, some less. Some living beings – and their number is considerable – are stricken by incurable diseases which lead to their untimely deaths.

The logical conclusion would be that all these noxious factors need to be eliminated.

Nevertheless, the economical, political and defense agendas are so powerful – often exaggerated – that our legitimate attempts in this direction become unrealizable.

How can one close down the chemical factories, if the government, as well as their owner, have invested huge sums in their development?! How can one force the politicians, who are preparing for military aggression or defense – to stop the nuclear experiments?

There is, nevertheless, a promising start: more and more ecological organizations for the protection of the environment are being created. Some of them are internationally recognized and they have a worldwide influence.

In this hostile and polluted environment, only by functioning as a complete, perfectly lucid man, in a state of inner harmony, can we help the body kickstart its physiological and organic mechanisms of adaptation. All-encompassing Attention is the only instrument integrating us into the alive, active and real present, uniting us with the Cosmic Energy.

All-encompassing Perception and the "Ego"

Life must be approached through a direct contact,
The whole being is wide open;
Neither past, nor future,
Absolute simplicity is the path.

Just listen and watch, with a total Attention:
Thoughts, images, desires, the illusions of the ideal mind,
The automatic movements of thought,
Created by time, as a possessive, arrogant "ego".

Everything we encounter – an all-encompassing
                                      perception –
Immediately disappears, it vanishes completely,
Without resorting to will, force or imagination;
A natural consequence of spontaneous action.

The all-encompassing observation of the reactions
                                      of the mind
Effortlessly ends any movement of the "ego";
The state of "psychological void" ensues:
Inner peace and stillness – as a complete "Whole".

In that moment of "emptiness" – expanding, boundless,
We have a new mind and a different way of thinking;
New brain cells start to function,
We are united with all that Life brings.

The "ego", based on what is old and outdated,
Is suddenly eliminated;
In the new dimension, the past disappears,
All the misguided conditioning.

Free from the past – psychologically – we are freshness,
Encompassing the freshness of Life – a perfect
                              comprehension;
The whole secret of Happiness lies in this direct contact,
Integrated into the present, as a whole being.

In order to correctly understand Life in Its general unfoldment, as newness and freshness from one moment to another, we need to encounter It with the same qualities that It has.

We need to welcome Life with a completely open being, through a direct contact. Neither the past, preserved in the memory, nor the future participate in this simple encounter. We just listen and watch – with an all-encompassing Attention – everything that appears automatically on the surface of our consciousness: thoughts, images, desires, fears, emotions etc. triggered by the impressions coming from the external world or from within our being. These outdated and inadequate apparitions – as "ego" in action – are completely dissipated by the rays of the Light-Attention.

Practically, this simple perception of the movement of Life in all its manifestations ends our whole conditioning, without any acts of will on our part. In the empty space that ensues, a "psychological void" appears; in its climate, we experience: peace, harmony and a total independence from our whole accumulated knowledge.

This is the moment of all-encompassing perception, determined by our encounter with Life; we have a new mind and a different way of thinking; new brain cells – unaffected by previous experiences – start to function. From now on we fully understand and embrace Life, eliminating any traumas or conflictual states.

In this fortunate circumstance, the "ego" – based on old, outdated cells – is instantly dissipated, as well as its energies and erroneous mentality.

Free from the past, we are eternal freshness and we have the ability to encompass and understand the freshness of Life in a real way.

The secret of unconditional happiness – to which every living being aspires – lies in this direct contact with the movement of Life, as a whole being integrated into the eternal present.

Work

It is not based on effort or struggle, with imaginary
                                                effects,
Led by the limited "ego" and the thinking process.
Work is a natural movement in our journey through life,
In such a state of existence, the Aliveness reveals its
                                                meaning.

Work is necessity, integrated psychologically
                                and physically,
It is not duality, created by the fragmented being.
Through it, the meaning of our life is legitimized
As a sacred duty – all is encountered in the human being.

The master of this world fulfills his holy purpose,
Manifested within himself as well as in his surrounding
                                                environment,
Affirming himself wisely, not recklessly and selfishly,
Nor overwhelmed by laziness and lethargy.

Choosing a certain profession, we pursue our potential,
Work becomes joy, for we are integrated into it.
We fulfill it with ease, working for the sake of work,
Not pursuing any purpose or goal, nor performing it
                                                out of fear.

We don't pursue any reward, work is a reward in itself,
The fruit of today creates the tomorrow.
When we work with love, we use small amounts of
energy,
We perform it well, in complete harmony.

To the lazy, it is a burden, a ceaseless drag,
In all they do, they resist and assess – their effort is
anguish.
Spiritually, work is immediately rewarded,
For, in each moment, we discover Happiness.

Work is a necessity required by the very existence of the Aliveness. It is justified by the immutable law of universal movement. Lack of movement, on any level of life, can only lead to progressive degradation and, eventually, to an untimely death. As such, movement and life are in permanent and close connection.

The evolution of the incarnated Aliveness can only be attained through work, directed by intelligence. In this sense, work finds its reason of manifestation through clarity and precision. Only in this circumstance will we be able to discover the true meaning of life.

From microorganisms to human beings, work manifests itself in its countless aspects. The plant rotating its flower, following the movement of the sun, the ant running tirelessly from dawn till dusk, the majestic vulture flying high in the sky – all perform activities required by their very existence.

Work, in the real sense of the word, is not an obligation imposed by someone else, nor is it forcedly imposed by our thinking process. In both instances the individual is forced to make an effort, a physical or intellectual strain, in order to conform to an inner or outer will. In this circumstance, because work is the effect of a command or an obligation, it will be followed – as an automatic effect – by frustrations and contradictory psychological reactions. When we approach it in this manner, work becomes a burden, with negative emotional effects and a huge waste of energy, finally resulting in tiredness, bitterness and suffering.

Because work is in close connection with life, our attitude towards work needs to also have the quality of simplicity. Therefore, the "ego" is completely excluded from this encounter. Completely integrated in the moment psychosomatically, we will welcome everything that the movement of life brings, without opposing any resistance. As whole beings, with a pure energy, the joy of work comes as a natural consequence. When we function as a whole man, the energy needed for work will be imperceptible. The qualitative and quantitative result of work will be at the highest level.

Choosing the right profession has become very important. We are born with certain aptitudes and talents; they are, in fact, echoes of certain occupations we performed in our past lives. If we pursue them, we will continue something that is already known and well preserved in the deeper levels of our consciousness. In this context, work will result in satisfactions and successes which are easy to attain.

Let us mention another circumstance, frequently encountered in the unfoldment of life. For external reasons, independent from our will, we must perform certain types of work that we are unprepared for or even feel aversion to.

How can we overcome this hurdle? Only in one way: by dissipating the reactions of the "ego". We simply encounter any fear of not knowing or any aversion towards this type of work in a direct, simple and immediate manner, with our whole Attention; this encounter dissipates any reactions. In the silence that ensues as the "ego" is dissipated, we are enveloped by a pure energy, manifesting itself as Intelligence and Love. From now on, we will solve our problems by other means than those of the ordinary thinking mind; joy accompanies us in everything we do.

For lazy people, work is a burden and it destroys the state of apathy they indulge in. They measure and assess everything, dragging their existence, constantly striving for something else that they wish to obtain for free or without any great intervention on their part, if possible. In thought, speech or deed, this negative attitude shapes their existence and has negative consequences both on themselves and on their surrounding environment. Always discontent and obstructive, they are never in syntony with the moment.

The Simplicity of the Encounter with "What Is"

Psychologically, we approach Life with all our feeling,
Although simple, this wondrous encounter is difficult;
Simplicity is not the problem, only the restless mind,
Conditioned by time, by words and knowledge.

It is an unsurpassable obstacle in the encounter with
"what is",
Therefore, knowledge and the "ego" – with all its story –
must be silent!
If mind and thought are silent – the human being is
liberated,
Without desire and expectations, we discover true Life.

In a state of freedom – through "Self-knowing",
We expand into Infinity – melting with the Sacred.
We encounter Love, transforming everything;
In Its absence, there is only chaos and calamity.

Does the mind become silent by itself, so we can be
Simplicity?
Of course it doesn't, for it is "ego" and activity!
Only Light-Attention can make the mind become quiet,
It dissolves its energies and It dissipates the known.

In the "emptiness" that naturally ensues, revealing itself,
Simplicity and Truth transcend us into Infinity.
Thus we discover our own Perfection,
"One" with Divinity, in constant movement.

What prevents us from truly encountering this eternal "what is" – whatever Life brings us as an effect of our destiny, which we ourselves created in a distant past? These two words are very easy to understand: simplicity and encounter. Yet actually fulfilling this reality is so difficult! The problem is neither simplicity nor the encounter. The main reason why this phenomenon is difficult to accomplish is the individual mind, which accumulates knowledge in the form of images; reacting automatically, it distorts the understanding of the reality of "what is".

As we discover and shatter this obstacle, by ourselves we understand what needs to be done: the whole mind baggage must be silent! It is only when the past has disappeared that we are liberated beings, able to encounter true Life.

Does the mind become silent if we desire or order it to be silent? Of course not, because its roots lie in the astral brain, connected with the physical world through the physical brain; its essence is repetition.

Confronted with all these automatisms of the mind, the only solution at our disposal is lucid, all-encompassing Attention. The simplicity of the encounter between Attention and the reactions of the mind makes them disappear instantly; simultaneously, the knowing mind dissolves. In the "psychological emptiness" that ensues, we have a new mind, expanding into Infinity, integrating us into the eternal newness of the Aliveness in perpetual movement.

This true psychological death of the past enables the simple encounter with whatever the movement of Life brings us; it also transcends us from the finite world into Boundlessness. In this state, we discover that we are an immortal being – Divinity in its essence – and that we were never separated from the Source of all Sources, the Unique Reality permeating and overflowing onto the whole creation through outpourings of Love and hallowing Grace.

Peace

Peace, absolute silence as a blessing,
A priceless treasure with hallowing effects,
Cleansing and transforming the conditioned being,
Free from the possessive past, created by false beliefs.

We truly encounter peace when the turmoil is dissipated,
"Self-knowing" is the path leading to integration;
All-encompassing Attention
Shatters duality, revealing Oneness.

From now on, the true man, body and mind as one,
Understands true Life, through a direct experience;
There are no problems, no conflicts,
All is crystal clear, comprehended spontaneously,
                              when I encounter myself.

Moments unfolding, in permanent renewal,
Attract me, through melting, into one single movement;
Only thus can we comprehend the Aliveness, eternal
                                        freshness,
We and the Aliveness are "One" – in perfect harmony.

He who experiences this state is a perfect guide,
Beneficial to the world and to himself, moment to
                                        moment;
A true, Universal Man,
Radically transformed, expanding into Boundlessness.

By experiencing this Consciousness-peace,
We attain Enlightenment, a supreme fulfillment;
Through It, we are Love and supreme Happiness,
Free from any imaginary support.

Peace or the silence of the soul is a state of natural serenity;
our whole being is in harmony. In this blissful state, any
activity of the thinking mind is completely excluded; there
are no expectations and the body functions naturally, at its
full capacity, as far as breathing, digestion, blood circu-
lation, excretion etc. are concerned. It self-regulates any
dysfunctions and provides optimal conditions for self-

healing, even in the case of diseases deemed by doctors as incurable.

On a psychological level, this inner harmony is a true blessing; it creates a radical transformation by eliminating the dysfunctional energies of the time-space conditioning.

We cannot attain this state of psychosomatic equilibrium through any activity of the mind, such as a goal or an ideal. In fact, this is what humanity has been doing since very ancient times: pursuing the peace of the soul through various methods, concepts, theories, beliefs, repeating formulas etc.

"Self-knowing" has nothing in common with any of these practices. It gives us peace from the very beginning, from the first moment we apply it. With the help of spontaneous, lucid and all-encompassing Attention, we simply encounter what is not peace: that is, any turmoil, such as a thought, image, desire, fear etc. The simplicity of the encounter dissipates it instantly. In the "psychological emptiness" or the state of no-mind, our whole being is united as "One", functioning as a Whole – body, mind and spirit – in perfect union with the Aliveness in Its perpetual movement. From now on we move in syntony with Life, and all the problems connected to our existence are understood and solved straight away, in the happiest way possible.

By moving in perfect synchronicity with the Aliveness, from one moment to another, in perpetual freshness, the residues of the past – which brought us to our current incarnation – are eliminated, without any intervention on our part.

Through his very existence, such a liberated person represents a living example and a guide for his fellow beings.

Thanks to this manner of approaching Life, by experiencing the Universal, the practitioner creates the foundation for a new world, completely different from the one we live in at the moment (limited and led by an egoistic center).

By directly experiencing this inner serenity – with the help of Attention – we live in a state of Pure Consciousness and Pure Love, creating radical transformations within our whole being.

One day, no one can foretell when, we will encounter a surprise phenomenon: Enlightenment or Liberation. Postponing or accelerating this priceless realization depends on the determination of each practitioner, as well as on the mass of ancestral residues which brought us to reincarnation.

About the Author

Ilie Cioara was an enlightened mystic who lived in Bucharest, Eastern Europe. His writings in 16 books describe the experience of meditation and enlightenment, as well as the practice of Self-knowing using all-encompassing Attention. Like Ramana Maharshi, Krishnamurti, Eckhart Tolle, his is a simple message of discovering our inner divine nature through the silence of the mind.

The author's description of enlightenment, in his own words:

I was 55 years old. One morning, waking up from my sleep, I noticed that, psychologically, I was functioning differently from the night before. The mind had lost its usual turmoil. In a state of serenity I had never felt before, I was functioning in perfect communion with my whole somatic structure.

Only after a couple of hours I realized what had happened to me, without pursuing this "something" as an ideal to accomplish. I was, to use a simile, in the situation of a man blind from birth, who had just gained his sight after undergoing surgery. Everything around me was as new. I had an overall perspective on things. A silent mind allows the senses to perceive things as they are.

Through silence, the mind in its totality had become an immense mirror in which the outside world was reflected. And the world I was perceiving directly through my senses revealed its own reality to me. My fellow beings, close friends or complete strangers, were being regarded indiscriminately, with a feeling of love I had never felt before.

If any reaction of the mind surfaced, it disappeared immediately in contact with the sparkle of impersonal Attention. A state of quiet and all-encompassing joy characterized me in all circumstances, whether pleasant or painful. My behavior was that of a simple witness, perfectly aware of what was happening around me, without affecting my all-encompassing state of peace.

The State of the Sublime is, of course, difficult to describe, but not impossible to experience by someone who authentically practices awareness. In order to communicate it, a simple and direct language is used, which is not filtered through reason, because the "ego", with its subjective perception, is no longer there. To put it this way: the psychological emptiness is the one who lives the present moment, expresses this encounter into words and still remains present and available to the next moment.

Also Available

Ilie Cioara

The Silence of the Mind

***

*The Wondrous Journey
Into the Depth of Our Being*

Coming Soon

Ilie Cioara

I Am Boundlessness

Published by O-Books
www.o-books.com

BOOKS

O is a symbol of the world, of oneness and unity. In different cultures it also means the "eye," symbolizing knowledge and insight. We aim to publish books that are accessible, constructive and that challenge accepted opinion, both that of academia and the "moral majority."

Our books are available in all good English language bookstores worldwide. If you don't see the book on the shelves ask the bookstore to order it for you, quoting the ISBN number and title. Alternatively you can order online (all major online retail sites carry our titles) or contact the distributor in the relevant country, listed on the copyright page.

See our website www.o-books.net for a full list of over 500 titles, growing by 100 a year.

And tune in to myspiritradio.com for our book review radio show, hosted by June-Elleni Laine, where you can listen to the authors discussing their books.

MySpiritRadio